STEPHEN JONES

STEPHEN JONES

A THINKING MAN'S GAME: MY STORY

STEPHEN JONES
WITH SIMON ROBERTS

MAINSTREAM
PUBLISHING

EDINBURGH AND LONDON

This edition, 2010

First published in Great Britain in 2009 by
MAINSTREAM PUBLISHING COMPANY
(EDINBURGH) LTD
7 Albany Street
Edinburgh EH1 3UG

ISBN 9781845966942

A catalogue record for this book is available
from the British Library

Typeset in Caslon and Century Gothic

Printed in Great Britain by
CPI Cox and Wyman Reading RG1 8EX

Thanks to my family, Gwen and her family, and my friends for all their support during my career. To Duncan Sandlant, my manager and friend, for all his patience and the sound advice he has given me over the years. To my teammates and coaches and the medical staff who it has been a privilege to work alongside, and without whom none of what I have achieved would have been possible. A special thanks to the Scarlets and Clermont supporters for their loyalty, and to all Welsh rugby supporters, who have always been there, through thick and thin.

Thanks to Simon Roberts, for all his hard work and for being available at the drop of a hat on our tour through the coffee shops, cafes and restaurants of Wales.

Thanks to Huw and Ben at Huw Evans Picture Agency and Dan at Inpho Sports Photography for the use of some great photographs, and thanks to Graeme Blaikie, Deborah Warner and Kate McLelland at Mainstream for their time and patience in putting this book together.

CONTENTS

FOREWORD
BY MARC JONES

Stephen and I are brothers. He was born when I was five and a half years old, and growing up we spent a great deal of time in each other's company – almost always playing sport. As soon as Stephen could stand, I would ask him to kick a sponge tennis ball towards me in our living room, so that I could practise my goalkeeping. I guess kicking started early for him.

As we grew older, the games became more competitive and we would play for as long as possible. When it got dark in the back garden, we would turn the lights on in the house so we could keep playing and use any torches to hand. Failing that, we would take the ball indoors – needless to say, Mum's ornaments never lasted long!

Stephen has always been a talented sportsman, achieving representative honours in cricket, football and athletics. But it was in rugby that Stephen most wanted to succeed and, from 16 onwards, that is where his sporting energies were channelled. Around the same time as Stephen signed his first professional contract with Llanelli, I embarked on a PhD in sport psychology and, as a sport psychologist, it has been fascinating to observe his success from the perspective of someone who is interested in what it takes, mentally, to succeed at the highest level.

Stephen shares many qualities with other elite athletes. He is incredibly determined, and this determination to succeed pervades his lifestyle, his attitude to training and playing, and how he responds when the going gets tough. He is a perceptive person and, having observed what it takes to succeed, he has certainly grown less tolerant of mediocrity as he has grown older.

Like other elite athletes, Stephen has talked about how this determination comes from a fear of failure. However, fear of failure is only one part of the story. Some sportsmen and women never truly fulfil their potential because they are afraid to fail, while others, like Stephen, use the fear of failure as a stimulus to realise their full potential and attain real and sustained success. This is not just a play on words; the distinction is crucial and provides the basis for an enjoyable and successful career. As a rugby player, success can come in different forms and, while fame, money and adulation are nice, Stephen has always considered it important to gain the respect of his fellow players and coaches. He is also acutely aware of the history, tradition and standing of the teams he has played for at club, regional and national level and he cares about being part of a group of players who deliver success for these teams.

Of course, there are difficult moments in the careers of all sportsmen and women, and Stephen's is no exception. Indeed, his senior international career for Wales began in the 1998 game against South Africa in Pretoria. Wales were without a host of first-choice players, who were missing through injury, but Stephen gained his first senior international cap. I remember the build-up to the game and discussing the match with Dad beforehand. Despite Wales not having won a single game on the South African leg of the tour, we fervently believed that Wales would win. This supremely insightful analysis was followed by a 96–13 demolition. Like many other Welsh rugby fans, we had (and still have) the incurable optimism that no matter what the circumstances maybe, just maybe, Wales can win.

It was great to see Stephen establish himself in the Welsh team and I vividly remember the game against Ireland in 2000 when

Stephen scored his first try for Wales. I was at the far end of the field from the action, but it gave me the perfect perspective of the try. I saw Stephen collect the ball outside the 22 and break the first tackle. As soon as he did, he accelerated comfortably away from the covering Irish defender and it was obvious he was going to score. So often tries happen in an instant, but on this occasion I knew my brother was going to get the try for Wales and I could really savour the moment. Even discovering that the covering Irish defender Stephen so comfortably outpaced was the veteran second row Mick Galwey did nothing to dampen the memory.

Welsh rugby as a whole did not get to grips with professionalism as quickly as other countries, and the structure and environment left Welsh players ill-prepared to compete at the highest level. It was very difficult to see someone close work so hard to achieve so little, and at times it seemed as though this would never change. Yet Stephen never lost his faith that things would improve. He kept telling me that the Welsh squad were working really hard; he could see the progress in training and in games and he was convinced the good times were around the corner.

When Wales won the Grand Slam in 2005, I was so pleased for him. I knew how hard he, and the rest of the team, had worked to make it happen in the face of disappointing results. Of course, the Grand Slam did not lead to continued success and when Stephen was captain of Wales the results were not good.

During this time, Stephen was singled out and subjected to a sustained period of personal criticism in certain sections of the media. This was a difficult time for him. He loved playing for Wales, and he wanted to be captain and achieve success for them. Obviously, Stephen is not the only sportsman, let alone captain of Wales, to experience this, but it was tough to see him go through it all. It can be difficult to know what to say to someone in that position, but I do know Stephen deeply appreciated the support he received. I guess he would have expected support from his family and friends, but I know he was also very touched by the support he received from rugby fans in Wales and beyond through a number of letters and messages of goodwill sent to him at Stradey Park. It must have been a difficult period for Stephen, because during this time he actually looked paler than normal – something I had previously thought impossible! But instead of letting this experience knock his confidence and dampen his desire to play for Wales, Stephen responded by working hard to regain his Welsh place and contributed to the 2008 Grand Slam campaign. This is an example of the determination and resilience that is typical of him as a person and a player.

An autobiography often gives an insight into the person, not just the public persona. However, Stephen is really one of those people with whom 'what you see is what you get'. Whenever I think of Stephen, I smile, because when we are together we laugh a lot. He has a real zest for life. Admittedly, he can be guarded with the media, but the Stephen you see on the rugby field is a reflection of him as a person. He is intelligent, committed, fair, brave, proud, talented and good-humoured.

Writing this foreword has given me the chance to reflect on Stephen's career to date and, after doing so, I wanted to find a way of summarising his achievements and his qualities as a person. While league titles, Welsh Cups and Grand Slams are fantastic achievements, I always think his worth as a player can best be summed up by the fact that Gareth Jenkins, Graham Henry, Steve Hansen, Mike Ruddock, Sir Clive Woodward, Warren Gatland and Ian McGeechan have all selected him as their first-choice outside-half.

Being a rugby player, though, is only part of who Stephen is, and while I am very pleased for him that he has achieved so much success, most of all I am proud of him as a person. He has dealt with the roller-coaster ride of Welsh rugby without changing. He is the same humorous, generous and caring person he always has been, and that is, by far, his greatest achievement.

Marc Jones
September 2009

INTRODUCTION
BY SIMON ROBERTS

Who is **Stephen Jones?** That was the question an old friend asked me when I told her I had been asked to help write this book. It was a great question, one I hadn't even considered, but it resonated with me long after the cup of coffee in the Cardiff bar had gone cold. It was an incredibly perceptive remark and left me plundering my own memory banks for the answer for days, weeks, even months.

I had known Steve – or Jonesy, as most people know him – for more than a decade. He was somebody I respected, not because of his undoubted rugby intellect but because there was a brutal honesty at his very core. But who was he, really? Here was somebody who didn't crave adulation from the wider world, but respect from his peers. In fact, he was somebody who had positively shunned all the trappings and decoration that were on offer, or had been thrown at him, as Wales fly-half. It simply never interested him. It was always about achievement, not recognition.

It wasn't even about emulating all the greats who had worn probably the most famous shirt in world rugby (along with the New Zealand number 7), the Wales number 10 jersey. Those who sit in the stands, their living room, the rugby club or any bar where you watch a game, and even the professional cynics in the press box, will never truly understand what kind of pressure, even burden, that must be.

Let's reel them off: Carwyn James, Cliff Morgan, Dai Watkins, Barry John, Phil Bennett, Gareth Davies, Jonathan Davies and, of course, Neil Jenkins. That, surely, underlines what I am talking about. Don't get me wrong, Steve has always respected the great players who have gone before him and the mantle he inherited, but he simply, for whatever reason, never compared himself to any of those legends. He was simply Steve, or Jonesy, who had a job to do for his teammates. Doing the job for them was more important to him than living up to any kind of legacy bestowed upon him.

Even now, I am not sure he realises or appreciates who he is or what he has achieved. Two Grand Slams – only Bennett has won as many Grand Slams wearing the number 10 jersey for Wales – two Lions tours, three World Cups and 80 caps for Wales. He has captained his country and is the second-highest points scorer in the history of Welsh international rugby. His Test career has spanned more than a decade. Jonny Wilkinson, England's World Cup winner, even deferred to him and wore the number 12 jersey while Steve played fly-half for the Lions in New Zealand in 2005.

It requires a certain kind of humility, mental toughness, self-belief and sheer bloody-mindedness to be able to break your job down like that, and not get caught up in all the hype and expectation that surrounds Welsh rugby. The message was always simple and to the point: 'It's not about me, mate. It's about the team.' How many of us, in whatever job we do, have the ability to do that? I could reel off the good deeds he has done for people, which he has never publicised, that were above and beyond the call of duty, but it's simply not his style to say, 'Look at me.' I just hope when he swaps his boots for his slippers and the endless bowls of pasta for a rare steak, he allows himself the time to reflect on what he has achieved in a truly remarkable career.

Even in his darker moments, and there have been a few, he asked himself the searching questions before he challenged others. Then, while most of us would settle for the quiet life and blame everybody else, he would blame himself if he hadn't challenged the players and coaches around him and just settled for second best. It requires a certain type of courage to turn around and do that, but it also shows the respect you have earned when those very people listen to you. At times he even seemed to relish the tough times more than the success that came his way. Being written off, proving people wrong and diving deep into his own reservoir of resilience was, sometimes, the real battle that had to be won.

For me, that is why the Stephen Jones story is such a fascinating one to tell. Neil Jenkins, Ceri Sweeney, Gavin Henson, Iestyn Harris and James Hook have all competed with him for the Wales number 10 spot and he is still there. Even now I am not sure I have really got under his skin. After all, some truly talented rugby players have tried and failed, so what hope was there for yours truly?

All I know is that this is a bloke I would want next to me in the trenches and he would have no qualms in telling me if I had let anybody down. That is all you can ask. He is also bright enough to understand that you never give everything away – you have to keep something back for those you truly care about, but ultimately for yourself. For that, I have the utmost respect for him. There is a life outside rugby, even for a most passionate Welshman, and Stephen Jones is certainly that. He definitely appreciates, even in a rugby-mad country like Wales, that there is more to life. This is his story.

Simon Roberts
September 2009

CHAPTER 1

GRAV

Adversity doesn't build character, it reveals it.

– Vince Lombardi, legendary American football coach

On 15 November 2007, I experienced one of my toughest days on a rugby field ever. It wasn't facing the All Blacks, being captain of a Wales side beaten by a record score by England in Cardiff, or picking up the wooden spoon with the national team, it was being a pall-bearer at Ray Gravell's funeral at Stradey Park.

It was, and still is, a moment in my life that sums up rugby – a game I love and would play for nothing – but it also put it into perspective. God knows I hadn't done that in the early part of my career. I thought playing rugby was a matter of life and death. It pervaded everything I did, and defined me. Just being on the losing side after a game felt like the end of the world, but it never really was. It was only as I got older that I really appreciated that. Grav's funeral, though, did represent what the game, particularly in Wales, does for every community and for the country by bringing so many different people from different walks of life together. Rugby *isn't* a matter of life and death, and I do hope everybody appreciates that. Some things are much more important even than rugby.

Grav, as everybody knows, was somebody I loved. He wasn't just a Scarlets, Wales and Lions rugby legend, he was also a Welsh legend. Being asked by his wife, Mari, to carry his coffin at Stradey Park on that incredibly emotional day was one of the biggest honours in my life. Dwayne Peel, Simon Easterby, Gareth Jenkins, Delme Thomas, Derek Quinnell and I all carried him into the ground, which was Grav's second home. Even now I cannot describe the range of emotions I felt that day.

To see the place packed to the rafters with former Scarlets, Wales and Lions teammates of Grav's and a complete cross-section of the Welsh population, including great poets, singers and, of course, the very people who had taken him to their hearts – the Welsh public – was a fitting tribute to a great man. The funeral was shown live on television and Rhodri Morgan, the First Minister, was there. It was the closest thing we have had to a state funeral in Wales, but it was more than that for me. It was a day when all the people who loved this larger-than-life character could say goodbye to him and show how much they loved him, celebrating the incredible life of a great man.

I am not afraid to admit there were tears when I learnt about Grav's death, and keeping it all together on the day of his funeral was unbearably tough, but I just didn't want to let him down, or Mari and his two girls, Gwenan and Manon.

I can still remember taking the phone call at home from Stuart Gallacher, then Scarlets chief executive, who told me Grav had died. It completely floored me. I think his death came as such a shock because Dwayne Peel and I had been to see him in Glangwili hospital not long before and he had been in great form. He was his usual positive self, cracking jokes with us, his fellow patients and staff, and trying to put us all at ease. He was coming to terms with having his lower leg amputated due to diabetes, but you would never have known he had just been through the trauma of a major operation. All he wanted to talk about was rugby – the Scarlets and Wales – and our families. He hardly mentioned himself. That was Grav all over.

Here was somebody who had been one of our greatest ambassadors and he had passed away in Spain, miles away from the country he loved so much. Everybody thought he was on the road to recovery and had been amazed by his resilience after the operation. Nobody expected him to die. I fully expected to see him around Stradey and that he would always be on the phone, telling me some great story or handing out another great piece of advice. But he was gone, just like that. I couldn't believe I wouldn't talk to him or get one of his famous big bear hugs or giant pats on the back ever again. The sadness was overwhelming.

Grav and Peely went way back. Peely's grandfather, Bert Peel, was the Llanelli physio. He is a figure who has gone down in Stradey Park folklore. He used to play all sorts of mind games with Grav when he was in his pomp as a player, just to get him on the field. They were a real double-act, and Peely grew up with all the stories about how his grandfather would pass Grav fit to play. The most famous one I know is when Grav went down injured during a game, clutching his knee, and Bert ran on and immediately applied the ice-cold 'magic sponge' to Grav's head.

'It's my knee that's injured!' Grav said, pushing the sponge away.

'No, Ray, the injury is in your head,' Bert replied.

Grav always regaled us with stories during our visits – there were so many, you could probably publish a book full of them. I can still remember the way he dismissed two big wingers we were about to face in a game with a simple put-down: 'I have seen bigger wings on a blackbird.' It was said with the usual glint in his eye and a hint of mischief.

Grav was just one of those special people who, no matter what, had the rare ability to make you feel on top of the world or ten feet tall after you had talked to him. Even now I miss the big slap on the back that would nearly knock me off my feet, or bear hugs that would leave me gasping for breath. He was, quite simply, a one-off.

He loved people – not just rugby people – and loved life. He loved being Welsh and would make sure everybody knew he was proud to be Welsh, but he was never a parochial Welshman. Watching him do a post-match interview on TV with a non-Welsh speaker always brought a smile to my face. You could see the player or coach he was about to interview look on in absolute horror as he asked his question in Welsh, and then their absolute relief when he asked the same question in English.

Everybody knew Grav was a proud Scarlet. Of course, his 'West Is Best' catchphrase has gone down in legend and is emblazoned across one of the stands at the new Parc y Scarlets. People loved and respected him because he wanted everybody to do well – as long as you didn't beat his beloved Scarlets! He made no attempt to hide his bias towards the Scarlets and his heart-on-sleeve approach to life is what made him so popular.

I can still remember when Llanelli played the All Blacks in 1998 at Stradey and Grav, who had been part of the famous Scarlets side that had beaten New Zealand in 1972, walked into the dressing-room before kick-off to talk to all the players. He didn't say a word, just started crying and had to walk out. He came back moments later and the same thing happened again; it brought a smile to all the boys' faces and broke the tension, but it also showed how much the Scarlets meant to him.

He got a real kick out of being around coaches and players because it kept him in touch with the game he loved. The smell of liniment, sweat and tension in the dressing-room before a game was like a drug to him. He probably didn't realise it, but for me he was a very real link to the great history of the Scarlets. He might not have been the greatest player to play for the club, but he was the greatest Scarlet by a country mile. Whenever I step onto the field, I remind myself I am representing him and the other legendary players who have worn that famous and very special jersey. It is a responsibility I feel very deeply and take very seriously indeed.

When I was Wales captain – or anytime, for that matter, when I had felt the world was against me – Grav would always leave me the same message on my mobile phone, '*Ti yw'r gorau,*' which translated from Welsh into English means 'You are the best.' He almost had a sixth sense about when to leave a message; it would always be timed to perfection and was the ultimate pick-me-up. That was the kind of man he was. I don't think he ever knew how much that meant to me – and how much it would have meant, I am sure, to everybody to whom he did the same thing. It was something he didn't have to do, but he did it to make sure you knew he was thinking about you and that he was on your side.

Everybody knew he'd had more than his fair share of personal battles, but he never showed it if they caused him any kind of pain. He was such an incredibly positive person. He was always supportive and always looked for the good in everyone. One thing is for sure: the world is a poorer place without him.

Grav represented all that is good about rugby. He was passionate about the game and didn't want to let his teammates down. He would knock seven bells out of the opposition during the match but would always have a drink with them afterwards, whatever the result.

In my rugby career I have been so lucky to come across so many good people. The game may have changed out of recognition because of professionalism, but rugby does have its own set of unique values and I hope it never loses them.

Rugby is a team game and its team ethos and camaraderie are what make it so different from so many other sports. It's why I love the game. I would never have been any good as a tennis player or at any other individual sport. Snooker player Matthew Stevens is an old school friend of mine, and I have nothing but admiration and respect for him, but winning and losing on your own just doesn't appeal to me. I like to be part of a team, where you win and lose together. I love the banter, the constant mickey-taking and, as I get older, I even love the challenge of trying to build team spirit in a side that is struggling on the field.

Rugby's great appeal for me is that it teaches you to rely on the man next to you, and he, in turn, must be able to count on you in the heat of battle. It's a physical test, but it's also a test of your character, mental toughness, selflessness and honesty. Sometimes you have to take responsibility and some pain for your teammates; other times you have to challenge people around you and be big enough to have the same done to you.

One thing I have learned about the game as I have got more experienced is that there are no short cuts. If you want to be part of a successful rugby team, sometimes you have to go through a lot before you can taste victory. And the old cliché that you learn more from your defeats than from your victories is just so true. You learn more about yourself, your teammates and ultimately your team when things aren't going well. You might even find out things about yourself you didn't know and don't like. Sometimes you realise you are not as good as you think you are.

Scott Johnson, Wales's former skills coach, is another rugby man for whom I have huge respect and admiration. Johno is a typical Aussie and, just like Grav, a larger-than-life character. His arrival in Wales back in 2001 coincided with the beginning of my rugby education. Technically, he was outstanding. He taught me the basic principles of the game and how to implement them, and made me realise I knew so little about rugby, really. Before he arrived my approach was based around trial and error on the pitch. Johno opened my eyes to the different styles of rugby and showed me there was more than one way to skin a cat. He taught me to think outside the box and to ask myself the question: 'Why?' Why are we doing this? Is it because this is what we have always done, or is it because it is the right thing to do?

He made a big impression on how I thought about rugby and this had a dramatic effect on my game, but he made an even greater impact on me off the field. He taught me valuable lessons about achieving balance in my life outside rugby. Throughout my career, especially in the early days, I would have terrible mood swings if I lost a game of rugby. I would dwell on a defeat for days and be a real nightmare to be around. Johno has been touched by tragedy – he lost his first wife to cancer – and probably because of that he has got life, and rugby in particular, in perspective. He works hard, but knows where and when to take a break from the game. It doesn't have to be all-consuming. He would always have something else to talk about other than rugby. It might be a book he was reading, a country he wanted to visit, a film he had seen, the music he was listening to or another sport he followed. He taught me how to switch off from the game. Despite all that has happened to him, he is another incredibly positive and supportive bloke.

Rugby is the national sport of Wales and it can be overwhelming. I used to obsess about every little thing on and off the field. Johno managed to put all of that into context for me; he taught me how to forget about the Welsh rugby goldfish bowl and to stop seeing playing for my country as a burden and to enjoy and revel in the responsibility. He reminded me how lucky I was to be wearing the red jersey and how every man, woman and child in Wales wanted to swap places with me when I stepped out onto the field for those big games. He taught me to get away from the game and to get off the emotional roller coaster, to stop talking and thinking about it every minute of every day. I cannot tell you how important or valuable that has been to me. It has been the biggest personal challenge of my career.

I can still remember one of the best debriefs he ever gave was the morning after Wales had been beaten by 40 points by New Zealand in Cardiff in the autumn of 2005. We had been on the end of another heavy defeat, but would go on and beat Australia 24–22 at the end of the same autumn series for the first time in 18 years. He was facing a room full of Welsh players who were broken men, but he showed us video clips of all the things we had done well in the game and told us how we could inprove, and we walked out of the team room believing we could have beaten the All Blacks if we played them right there and then.

He outlined how much we had improved and how the performances were drastically better, and he backed it all up with footage, stats and facts. Nobody could argue with his analysis. I still don't know how he managed to change the attitudes of such a negative bunch of players into a team who believed we could be the best in the world. Incredible. But that was how positive and perceptive he was, and the type of belief he had in us. He didn't rip us apart because we had done this or that wrong, but told us what we had done well and then proceeded to explain to us how we were going to fix the mistakes. When somebody has that kind of belief in and knowledge of you, it is infectious and breeds self-belief within yourself and your team.

I have been very fortunate to play alongside some great players throughout my career, but even more fortunate to play alongside some great people. Tony Marsh, a teammate at Clermont, is somebody else who stands out and had a big impact on me. He is a New Zealander who had played for France and had adopted everything French. He is more French than the French – he just loved the lifestyle and approach to life. He was a typical Kiwi on the pitch, but so relaxed off it.

He also has a really refreshing attitude to life after having been diagnosed with testicular cancer early in 2003. Following some really aggressive medical treatment, he fought back from all of that trauma to resume his rugby career. Not only that, but months later he played for France in the 2003 World Cup in Australia and helped them reach the semi-finals of that tournament. He took me under his wing while I was playing in France and looked after me – he didn't have to do that.

Marshy did a lot of work for a cancer charity in Clermont and would visit sick children in the town's hospital, but he never made a big deal about what he was doing. He just related to the battles they were going through and wanted to give something back. He had been through a major operation and chemotherapy and was a classic example of what can be achieved with a positive attitude and outlook on life.

Don't get me wrong, Marshy could be brutal and wouldn't hold back if training had been bad, but he also knew that rugby was a game to be enjoyed and that winning and losing was part of the deal. He had all of that in perspective and knew missing a few kicks, a couple of tackles and losing a game wasn't the end of the world. Marshy wanted to win and trained as hard as anybody, but he knew when to let go and wouldn't dwell on victory or defeat. He knew all about the bigger picture, and I learnt a lot from him about just enjoying the moment.

There have been so many people from very different walks of life who have had a similar impact on me. There are too many to name but they have all, in their own way, been an inspiration to me. Rugby has been a massive part of my life and I have been lucky enough to meet so many really good people.

There is no secret recipe to being successful in rugby – it's just like life. Surround yourself with good people, work hard and be honest. It's about trust, self-belief and showing respect to others. If you have those ingredients in your life, you won't go far wrong in rugby.

CHAPTER 2

IN THE BEGINNING

One of the things that my parents have taught me is never listen to other people's expectations. You should live your own life and live up to your own expectations, and those are the only things I really care about it.

– Tiger Woods, winner of 14 Majors and 70 PGA Tours;
the youngest player to achieve golf's own Grand Slam

West Wales is different. It has its own pace of life and a culture all of its own. Growing up there was pretty idyllic and very sheltered, and my abiding memory of my childhood is as a very happy one. I played sport, any sport, wherever and whenever I could. I had a very classic Welsh upbringing, and it probably wasn't any different to any other boy's, living in any village, town or city in Wales. I went to a Welsh-speaking school but spoke English at home. There was a good cross-section of backgrounds amongst the kids at school, with sons and daughters of farmers mixing with townies. I am a Welsh-speaker, and very proud to be Welsh, but would like to think I have never been parochial or blinkered about my Welshness. My great-grandfather, Agostino, was from Naples in Italy. His son, Vincent, my grandfather, arrived in London before being stationed with the British Army in Newcastle Emlyn. Apart from my Italian roots, I am as Welsh as they come.

I was born in Aberystwyth in 1977, but moved to Carmarthen when I was very young and that has always been the place I call home. I have travelled the world as a rugby player, but my roots will always be there. My family and my friends have always been, and still are, very important to me. Rugby may be my career, but they are my life. They have been there for me during the good and bad times, but more importantly they are there at any time in my life. I hope they all appreciate how important that is for me.

My mother, Glenda, and father, Michael, split up when I was very young, but all my memories of growing up involve loads of family and friends. I certainly didn't feel different from any of the kids because my parents weren't together. My mum and dad have been very supportive of my career and have always been there for me, through all the ups and downs. My family has been the foundation of everything, especially any success I have enjoyed. We are a small family, but they have been the rock around which everything has revolved and we are very close.

I spent a lot of time with my grandparents growing up, and my life centred on Carmarthen. Even when I was playing for Wales, or when things were tough for me as captain, I have never locked myself away or hidden from the people of my home town. They are always supportive, wishing the team and myself well.

I do hope I have made my parents proud of what I have achieved as a rugby player and who I am as a person, though they do have very different ways of dealing with my career. My mum has travelled and seen the world because of rugby and has been there to see me play for Wales on tours, at World Cups and on Lions tours. My dad is the complete opposite and, although he has travelled to watch me play a few times, he gets very nervous and prefers to watch the game on TV in his living room at home, with the obligatory glass of red wine to calm his nerves, with my stepmother, Ann.

My brother, Marc, is five and a half years older than me and we always played sport against each other when we were growing up. We would always be kicking or throwing a ball in the backyard until it was dark or we were called in for supper. We have always been very competitive; it is a battle of survival playing any sport against a much bigger older brother. I always wanted to beat him, though he was usually good enough to change the rules to give me a better chance of winning because he was so much bigger and older than me. It certainly honed my competitive streak and forced me to look after myself, and it definitely helped create the well of stubbornness and determination I would dip into whenever I needed it, to be a success later in my rugby career. The ability to get up after being knocked down – or written off – was perfected on those dark nights in the garden playing against my brother. Marc has been constant and a great support throughout my career. If I ever need to get away or things start to get on top of me in Wales, I just jump in my car and go and see him and his wife, Helen. He has a great outlook on life and, being a sports psychologist, has a great take and genuine worldview on sport. But the bottom line is that he's my brother. He's still the first person I talk to if I am frustrated about anything, not just rugby. I have also had great support from my stepsister, Hayley, and my stepbrothers, Christian and Jamie.

Marc has been hugely important to me and is a big part of my success. I know he has enjoyed listening to my trials and tribulations, and those of Welsh rugby, and has often found my experiences coming to terms with the professional game hilarious. I can hear him now, saying, 'How can that go on in any professional sport?' But he has never interfered and has been a great sounding board for me. He has also helped me differentiate between the facts about what has been happening to me and somebody else's opinion, and that has been an invaluable tool for me.

Marc and Helen were both with me at Heath hospital before the World Cup in 2007 when I found out how serious my groin injury was. When I came out of the examination and told them the prognosis, Marc was more disappointed than me. Both were a great support then – but I was already thinking about how I was going to get fit and the work I needed to do to make the tournament.

My school days revolved around a ball – football, cricket or rugby. I was always kicking or throwing one as a youngster in Carmarthen. I would be in the yard before school started, and enjoy a kickabout every breaktime and lunchtime before having another after school.

Bro Myrddin was a working-class school at the centre of the community, with some really good core values that have stood me in good stead over the years. The ethos was, if you work hard, you will be rewarded. It was a very successful school academically but, ironically for me, it had no real sports or rugby tradition while I was there. Emyr Lewis, the flanker, and Mefin Davies, the hooker, who I've played alongside in World Cups and Six Nations, are the only other former pupils to be capped by Wales. Rugby wasn't really a major priority for anybody at school, but that has changed over the years. Young Scarlets such as Rhys Priestland and Ken Owens, Aled Thomas, who played for the Dragons, and Wayne Evans, who is with them now, all went to the same school as me.

I do remember one teacher, Hefin Elias, who played a lot of football and brought a real focus on passing to the rugby team. He brought the same passing discipline he used in football to his rugby coaching. He had a real understanding about space. It was something that would become a central part of my make-up as a professional rugby player years later.

Garan Evans's father, Wyn, who coached the Wales Under-18s, had a very similar philosophy. He was a physical education teacher at Stradey Comprehensive and wouldn't allow any of his players at school to kick the ball during a game: they always had to pass and run with the ball. I have always identified with that approach to the game and think it is a brilliant philosophy for youngsters to have growing up playing rugby.

It's probably heresy for a boy from West Wales to admit that as a schoolboy football was my first love and that my first sporting hero was Ian Rush. I know it should probably have been a Scarlet legend like Grav, Phil Bennett or Ieuan Evans, but a football ground called Anfield was much more important to me than Stradey Park when I was a kid. Marc was a mad Liverpool fan and, like any younger brother, I did whatever he did and so was a big Reds supporter, too. The two of us used to wear our Liverpool football kits, with the famous Crown Paints logo on the front, almost religiously. I can still remember how distraught I was when Rushie, who was a Welsh legend to the pair of us, signed for Juventus in Italy.

I came into rugby late, and I didn't really start playing properly until I was fifteen, though I had played for Carmarthen District when I was between ten and eleven. Up until then, it had all been football. I played central midfield for my county football team and even captained the side, while as a teenager I made a Wales development squad.

I played for Bro Myrddin and the district team, but it was all about playing alongside my mates, really. Thoughts of playing rugby for Wales in the Five Nations, as it was then, didn't even enter our minds. We just wanted to score against each other. I certainly didn't have any ambitions about playing rugby for Wales or running out at the Arms Park against England, or anything like that.

While I played football during the winter, over the summer months it was cricket. I would spend most of my time at Carmarthen Wanderers cricket club trying to get to grips with a cricket bat and ball. I really fancied being one of my England cricket heroes at the time, Graham Gooch and David Gower. I was playing in the Wanderers 'Firsts' when I was 14, which was full of grown men, and would bat and bowl a bit. I loved cricket, mainly because of the mental strength and concentration you need to play the game. Cricket is a really tactical game and I think that was the appeal for me. The Wanderers were just one of those great local clubs that had a thriving junior section and great facilities. I don't get down there as much as I should because of rugby commitments and being on tour, but even now I always look out for their results and try to check to see where they are in the table.

Aged 15 I had the chance to play rugby for the Wales Under-16s and that is when rugby really started for me. It was my first experience of travelling back and forth to training in Cardiff from Carmarthen and I felt that I was part of something special at the time. We only played one game that year, when we travelled up by coach to Twickenham to play against the old enemy. It was my first real taste of that rivalry with England. It was also the first time I had been in a team where you were given a free kit and had back-line moves in a game. The honour of playing for my country really hit home for me – and at rugby's HQ.

I played fly-half and we drew the game, and I had been bitten by the rugby bug. After that game, I really started to take my rugby seriously. A whole new world had opened up to me. Not many of that Wales Under-16 side actually made the grade in first-class or professional rugby, although Leon Lloyd, the former Leicester and England wing, was part of the England Under-16s that day in London.

I had been exposed to a really high level of sport and, for me, it just got the juices going. I didn't have any grand ambitions at that stage of my career; I just enjoyed playing the sport. At the time, there were no pathways or academy to pick you up, nurture you and develop your talent. It was all about playing a game you enjoyed and it didn't really feel overly competitive. I just kind of got swept along in it all. The only rugby I watched on TV was the Five Nations and I would go along to Stradey Park for the odd game every now and then. You would be hard-pressed to say I was any kind of rugby fanatic at that age, but my first experience of the real passion of grassroots rugby in Wales came soon after.

I was playing for Carmarthen Quins Youth, coached by my

father's friend, Spencer Jones, in a local derby against Carmarthen Athletic. My dad was an Athletic supporter, along with my uncle Lyn and auntie Del, and there would always be some good banter before and after the game. A crowd of about 1,500 would turn up to watch this local derby at the 'Bowl' in town and it was always a great occasion. Players from the same school teams would be on opposite sides and there was a massive rivalry – it was all about who would have bragging rights after the game. It was classic Youth rugby in Wales at the time. All the boys would be dressed up in the regulation white shirt, club tie and chinos after the game for a night on the town to celebrate a great victory or to console themselves after a defeat. They were great times. Clubs like Quins and Athletic are the bedrock of our national game. I hope nobody ever forgets that.

It's only much later that you really appreciate the time and care people put in to allow youngsters to play sport at that level. I am always amazed by the volunteers who give up their free time so others can play sport. How many of us do that now? They would be up at 9 a.m. on a Saturday morning marking out the pitches for the rugby and football teams, and they did it all for nothing. One gentleman in particular, come rain or shine, would mark out the pitches for us. Nobody saw him doing it, and he probably got no thanks for it, but he did it for his community and because he knew others would enjoy themselves later in the day. Unbelievable. There are so many good people like him. I am always aware that without people like him I may never have been given so many opportunities later in my career. I have always been very conscious of where I come from and there are so many things like this that I can draw on. Motivation has never been a problem for me because I know how lucky I am, and have been, to represent the town and country that made me. I have never forgotten, nor will I forget, that I am in a privileged position.

I still have the same friends I had growing up. They have been a constant support and have kept my feet on the ground. Rugby can be all-consuming, but I still make a point of going on holiday every year with the same boys I grew up with, though now instead of 'boys only' holidays, we take our girlfriends, wives and kids with us. I wouldn't have it any other way. I don't think they truly appreciate how much I enjoy and cherish the time away with them. They never allow me to get 'big-time' or carried away with myself: I am just Steve. They don't treat me any differently now from when I was just a boy growing up in Carmarthen. We hardly ever talk rugby and that is the way I like it. Usually, the only time they ever mention it is to ask for a handful of tickets or to bag me for some mistake I have made on the pitch. I am the one who usually cops the most flak and abuse.

Most of the 'Boys y 'Bro' are high-achievers, having gone into medicine and law, and all are very successful in their own right. I was dragged along in their slipstream when I was at school; they were all ambitious and driven and wanted to be the best at their chosen profession, and I just really picked up on that. I can remember when everybody was studying for their exams, I was the one asking if anybody wanted a kickabout. But because they were studying, I did the same thing. They were a good influence on me, and still are. We have a shared history and have so many other things to talk about. Since rugby is never high on the agenda, being with them always allows me to completely switch off from the game. They have never allowed me to dwell on a defeat or let me get carried away with a victory. If I have done something badly on the field, they will rip me apart for it and if I have done something well, they remind me of the bad things I have done playing rugby. I can't win. I may be the butt of most of the jokes, but I can hold my own, don't worry about that. We are a normal group of friends who rip each other mercilessly but would do anything for each other.

I can remember when I was selected to play for Wales against

Ireland at the Millennium Stadium in 2001 and everybody wanted tickets for the game. I was told in no uncertain terms to sort it out. I managed to get enough tickets to keep everybody satisfied, but we played so badly that day that everybody refused to pay me for getting the tickets. It cost me about £200! A great party had been planned for watching the rugby, and they all enjoyed telling me what a great day they had had. I was nursing the bumps and bruised pride of a heavy defeat – then had to suffer the ultimate humiliation. They had a great get-together, drinking in the pubs and clubs of Cardiff, while I was at work.

Being a rugby player in Wales can be overwhelming and I am very aware of that. Players can become cocooned in a very unreal world where everybody you know and every connection you have is linked to the game. With all the media hype now surrounding the game, it does mean it's hard to switch off. There are some players who have rugby at the centre of everything; I was probably the same when I was younger, but I have got less and less comfortable with that as I have grown older. I want to be grounded and have tried to get the balance right.

As a rugby player in Wales, you are in the spotlight and doors do open for you, there is no doubt about that. I appreciate I play a sport that has a massive effect on the mood of the nation, win or lose, but I am a rugby player, not a doctor. I don't save people's lives. In the bigger scheme of things, rugby players aren't that important. If I ever feel I am getting swallowed up by the rugby machine, I ring one of my friends, catch up with them or go and stay with them. They are a great escape and release for me and always put things back into perspective.

I had played a couple of junior games for Carmarthen while I was still in school before I was asked to join Llanelli. The game was amateur back then, but when the club rang the school and asked if I was available to play, I couldn't believe it. This was something completely different – this was a first-class club that played touring teams and had a host of internationals in the starting line-up. I thought it must have been a joke, but I turned up and lined up alongside Welsh internationals Rupert Moon and Tony Copsey, those two great West Walians from the Midlands and London. I played in the centre and made my debut for Llanelli against Maesteg on a wet Wednesday night in February 1996. Kevin Ellis, who had just returned from a successful career playing rugby league in the north of England, played scrum-half for Maesteg that day. I was a boy in a man's world. I don't really know how the club found me, but I was captain of Wales Schools' Under-18s, coached by Wyn Evans, and he must have had a word with Gareth Jenkins, the Llanelli coach, and I guess he took a gamble on me. I was a teenager, and he must have wanted to have a look at me and see if I was made of the right stuff to play for him. I didn't ask any questions and did what I was told. I just didn't want to make a fool of myself or let anybody down.

I later found out that none of the senior players had wanted to play in the game, but at the time I just couldn't believe my luck. I was in the same side as players I had only ever watched on TV. I was hooked. When I was handed a brown envelope after the game by Anthony Buchanan, the Llanelli team manager, I was dumbfounded. I was 18 years old and was too scared to look inside. I got home, opened it and there was £25. I was astonished. I felt like a millionaire. I would have paid to play for the Scarlets. I can't really tell you how much it meant to me. It was massive. I had played for Llanelli! Whatever happened to me afterwards, nobody could take that away from me. I was as proud as punch, then went back to school the next day. Unbelievable. If my career had stopped there and then and never gone any further, I would have been happy. I even got an extra portion of dessert at school the following day because people had heard I had played rugby for their beloved Scarlets!

My career for Llanelli really started the following season, when I played in fly-half against Bridgend at the Brewery field, in the same side as Ieuan Evans, that Wales and Lions legend. I couldn't believe I was even allowed in the same side as him, let alone actually to play alongside him. I was in the starting line-up quite a bit that season and played from the bench, but I wasn't really a first-team regular or anything like that. I was a typical squad player, just learning the ropes, making mistakes and learning those tough lessons about what it took to play for Llanelli in first-class rugby.

Even at that stage, I hadn't any ambitions about playing for Wales, winning Grand Slams or joining a British and Irish Lions tour. If somebody had asked me, I would have laughed them out of court and called for the men in white coats. But all those games played against my brother and his best friend, Richard Davies, were of benefit to me when I started playing first-class rugby. I'd had to look after myself playing against Marc and 'Mad Rich' and it certainly toughened me up. I felt it gave me a real advantage when I started out on my rugby career.

I do really believe my upbringing, my family and my friends have had a major impact on my rugby career. I was brought up in a culture and environment where you had to look at what your weaknesses were if you wanted to improve. In my opinion, you cannot turn a blind eye to your weaknesses as a player, or a person. If you do that, you are never going to improve. I would like to think I am a pretty relaxed bloke, but my desire to improve and understand why things haven't worked is very important to me. I want to find out why I have done something or why I cannot do something and really analyse how to improve myself. I have always wanted to be as good as I possibly can – in my job and in my life. I have never had any problems admitting I have weaknesses and have never been afraid of them. Once you acknowledge them, you can sort things out. Knowledge is power. Finding the process to get better or improve is what rugby and life are all about. I don't hide from that.

Everybody has weaknesses in their game – no rugby player or sports star is the complete person. It's just impossible. You have to evolve every year because, if you don't, you will be left behind. I will be the first to admit that if things aren't going well, I get very pissed off. It means I am not doing my job properly. I will look at everything and sometimes pull everything apart – my training in the week, my match-day preparation – to find out why things aren't working. I focus and review everything. I know dropping a ball or missing a kick is part and parcel of being a fly-half, but if there is a real problem I notice it pretty quickly. I know I will make mistakes, but I want to make as few as possible. I need and want to know and be in control of why I am making those mistakes. I always find sports people who are flash in the pan or one-season wonders fascinating because they clearly haven't had a look at themselves and realised that they needed to work to improve. Those who play at the highest level for a period of time are the ones for whom I have the utmost respect. They have challenged themselves, improved and learned the lessons; they have acknowledged what they have to do to get better.

Professional sport is a ruthless business and the players who have a 'strawberry season' or one good year have simply not done their homework. For example, I see a young player who has had a good season and thinks he's made it, but he seems completely unaware of what happens next. The coaches, players and teams are now aware of him and his strengths, but, more importantly, his weaknesses. They analyse him like never before and come up with a plan to play away from his strengths and try to expose his weaknesses. You give him more attention and try to test him by running at him more often than you would normally, trying to tire him out so when he has the ball he is struggling with fatigue. How guys cope with difficult times has always fascinated me. If you stand still, you get left behind in this business. I have learnt to be open to new things and new experiences. That's why I went to play rugby in France.

I know the familiar picture of a Welshman is that he is a poor traveller and gets homesick whenever he steps outside Wales. I have never been like that and I like to think that is down to my upbringing. I love to travel and it is one of the real perks of being a professional rugby player. I have been lucky enough to visit some extraordinary places, but it does make you realise that Wales is a beautiful country and compares well with any of the fantastic countries I have played in, including places like France, Australia, New Zealand and South Africa. Rugby has opened my mind to the world, but also made me appreciate what I have on my own doorstep and how lucky I am. I don't know what I would be doing now without rugby. It has changed me as a bloke.

My girlfriend, Gwen, is the other big influence on me and doesn't let me get away with anything. She keeps my feet on the ground and has had to put up with a lot, being in a relationship with a professional sportsman. She has had to make sacrifices and has been patient with my moods when things haven't been great in my career, but she has also brought a real balance to my life. Gwen likes rugby, but doesn't have a similar obsession with the game. More importantly, she knew me before I was a rugby player. She helps me switch off from rugby. She has got me doing other things away from the game and has a great way of putting everything into perspective. I used to beat myself up whenever I'd lost a game and would carry it around with me for a couple of days. She taught me to switch off from the game – and that has become very important to me.

There were times in my life when rugby was the be-all and end-all. It literally *was* my life. Not any more. Gwen changed all that, thankfully. Now I can leave rugby at the front door, although I am sure Gwen would say I still watch too much sport on TV.

We had been together for five years from school before we split up in our early 20s and we got back together after I had returned to Wales from France. But it might never have happened had it not been for Dwayne Peel – I have him to thank for us getting back together again.

I'd had to withdraw from a Boxing Day game between the Scarlets and the Ospreys at the Liberty Stadium. I'd woken up suffering from some severe back spasms and had failed to run it off in the warm-up routine before kick-off. I had taken some painkillers in the changing room but was still walking like a duck. I was in agony and the medical decision was that I wasn't fit enough to play. I knew I would have been a passenger during the game, so I reluctantly agreed and sat out one of the great games in the Welsh rugby calendar. I wasn't a happy man. Like any Scarlet, playing the Ospreys is one of *the* games of the season.

Anyway, that night after the game, Peely had arranged to meet some friends in Carmarthen. Boxing Day is always one of the great nights in town because everybody is back for Christmas and it's when you get a chance to catch up with people. I was going to drop him off and then go home and rest my back up, but he kept badgering me to come in for a drink and in the end I agreed. My back was giving me some real gyp, but I said I would say hello and then go home. Being in a pub with people who've had a few drinks when you're sober is not something anyone really enjoys, but it turned into a really good night. Peely and I took some real ribbing because the Scarlets had lost and I was mercilessly ripped apart for missing out on the game. It had been billed as 'Jones versus Hook' and all that nonsense, and I'd had to withdraw at the last minute. As you can imagine, the boys enjoyed that one and wouldn't let it rest for one minute.

I was finally persuaded to have a beer and ignore the medical advice, and then I bumped into Gwen again. The rest, as they say, is history. I have Peely's persistence and persuasive powers to thank for that.

It's only as I have got older that I have truly appreciated how having a happy and stable personal life makes a real difference in my rugby career. I am happy at home and happy at work and those are the two key ingredients for success. I am a very lucky bloke because I have both. My family and my friends and my roots are what have moulded me and they are very important to me. They are the best support system I could have. Rugby cannot be the only thing in anybody's life, and it isn't in mine. Where do you go when you have your first setback in life? You go to your family and friends.

CHAPTER 3

LLANELLI AND
THE SCARLETS

The positive thing about local players is that they have
passion, and passion is contagious.

– Rafa Benítez, manager of Liverpool Football
Club and Champions League winner

When rugby union went professional, Llanelli offered
me a £10,000-a-year contract for three years and a Ford
Mondeo. It was like all my Christmases and birthdays
rolled into one. Newport and Swansea had both offered me a
professional contract, and I also had an offer to go to Loughborough
University to do a degree. I thought long and hard before deciding
what I wanted to do. It was a massive decision, and my parents
were incredibly supportive, but I knew deep down I wanted
to play rugby for a living and so I deferred the chance to go to
Loughborough for a year just in case rugby didn't work out. A
couple of years later, I tried to combine being a professional rugby
player with doing a sports-science degree at Swansea University,
but I soon gave that up.

With hindsight, I took a big gamble by not carrying on with my
education. It would have been hard to combine the two, but I was

living the dream and just wanted to soak it all up. I have nothing but admiration for the likes of my fellow Welsh teammates Alun Wyn Jones, Jamie Roberts and Leigh Halfpenny for mixing their studies with their international careers; they are great role models and a good example to any aspiring professional rugby player. During my two years in France, I saw how they encouraged young professional players to have something outside their rugby careers. Anyone who has his heart set on a career in the sport should remember it can be short-lived and can end in injury at any time. Make sure you have something else to fall back on. I didn't, and I was lucky.

Young rugby players tend to think they are superhuman and forget that nowadays a career lasts only a short time and can end so quickly. One of the most disturbing things I have experienced as a senior player is the sight of academy youngsters who have set their sights on becoming professional getting told they are being released and won't make it. They have usually thrown all their eggs in one basket and not even entertained the possibility they will not reach their goal. Seeing them distraught and worried about what they will do next, or what job they are qualified to do, is heartbreaking. It is the ruthless side of the professional sport. For every player who is lucky enough to wear the red shirt at the Millennium Stadium, there are so many more whose dreams have gone up in smoke. It's the harsh reality of the professional game – in fact, any professional sport – and the public rarely get to see that side of the business.

Some athletes feel to the manner born when they break into their particular sport, but I never felt that way and always knew I would have to work hard to make a success of my career. I would never describe myself as a naturally talented rugby player, rather I'm somebody who has worked hard and learned about what it takes to be a success. I would only realise how hard I would have to work nearly a decade later.

It took me a couple of years to feel part of the set-up at Llanelli because I was just in awe of the players and of Stradey Park. I was a teenager, just out of school, trying to make his way in senior rugby. I just kept my head down, worked hard and tried to show that I deserved to be there. It took me two or three years to really find my feet. Rugby at that level didn't come easily for me and I had to work hard before I could make a proper contribution to the team. Some of the verbal stuff on the field was a real eye-opener, really close to the bone.

I have never thought of rugby as being a job. Nowadays I do make a very good living from the game, but when I started out the sport was amateur. You just wanted to play for the best team in the area – and that was Llanelli. Young players have it very differently from me because there is a structure and there are stepping stones for you to become a professional. The young academy players coming through now are far, far better than I was when I started out. They are much further up the ladder than I was and understand they have chosen a lifestyle, not just a career or a job.

The game has become more ruthless, but also much more cosmopolitan and sophisticated as a professional sport. Three ex-Scarlets – Alix Popham, Barry Davies and Liam Davies – are playing, or have played, for Brive in France. Australians, New Zealanders, Tongans and Samoans have all been part of the Llanelli or Scarlets squad. Players in Wales only used to move around the first-class scene within the country and wouldn't even move to play in England – professional rugby has opened so many doors for players to experience different rugby cultures. The amateur days of being loyal to one club have gone because of professionalism. The game really has changed out of sight. A professional player knows he probably has ten years to make enough money to set himself up for a life after the game – that is the hard-nosed reality. Loyalty now has a price, like in any professional sport, and for players and clubs the game is a business. If he doesn't play well, every player knows he can be shown the door. Supporters, of course, want players to be loyal, but that is totally unrealistic when it is their livelihood. People change jobs in every walk of life and it is no different in professional rugby, though there have always been players, especially in Wales, who will play for their local side for much less than they could get at another club.

I know I have had the best of both worlds. I have seen the relaxed, amateur era, when you played and had a beer after a game, and I have worked at the very sharp end of the professional game, where I had the best of everything and my every need was catered for. In the amateur days, you played for enjoyment – just to be part of the side was enough. Winning was important, but it wasn't the be-all and end-all. Professional rugby is about winning, winning and winning. Nothing else matters. We are now in a results-driven business and that very business demands that you win. If a side wins rugby matches, it wins trophies, and then it wins prize money, boosts ticket and merchandise sales, and sponsors and commercial partners want to be associated with it. So everything the side does for 80 minutes on a Friday night or a Saturday or Sunday afternoon has a direct impact on the business of rugby and on the staff in the team shop and the ticket office.

When I first started to play for the Llanelli club side, before the game went regional in Wales in 2003, the business side of rugby was never a real focus, like it is today. We carried on like we had always done, but we were now paying tax and national insurance instead of getting our brown envelope at the end of every game. Nothing else had changed. Every club had a good social environment and we didn't really understand what being professional sportsmen, let alone professional rugby players, meant. We worked hard and played hard, but the penny hadn't really dropped at all. We were a million miles away from where we needed to be.

The Llanelli club I joined was like a big family, with everybody pulling in the same direction and for the cause. There were so many people – probably too many to mention them all – who played their roles in making the place what it was. There was Les Williams, the club statistician and historian, who knew everything about the history of the club and any records – appearances, points or tries – that were about to be broken. He was like an encyclopedia about the club, and still is. The late Bowen Stephen, the club treasurer, was another great character and he loved Llanelli and Stradey Park. He would always disturb my kicking sessions. He would come out of the tunnel with a cigar in his mouth, pushing a wheelbarrow and claiming he had my pay in it, and would ask me where I wanted him to put the wads of notes he was carrying in the bottom of it. There was Ann in the ticket office, who would always look after me if I needed to get some tickets for a big game coming up and would make sure I kept my friends and family happy. Then there was Wayne James, who I have always called 'the main man' because he kept the club ticking over, doing all the little things nobody really noticed to keep the club and the team going. He does anything, and everything, and is a real backbone of the place.

What I have always loved about Llanelli and the Scarlets, through the good times and the bad, is the team spirit. We have always had that, and it has been the foundation of every dressing-room I have been in. The banter has always been brutal, and some of the stuff that has gone on over the years is incredible. Someone would always be finding ice in a shoe, a pair of women's knickers in the pocket of their trousers, the end of his socks cut off or Deep Heat in his pants.

One of my favourite pranks was when we had to stay over in Bath after a Heineken Cup quarter-final at the Recreation was postponed until the following day due to a waterlogged pitch. I went to bed that night only to find the contents of my room's minibar were in my bed. But that was nothing compared to Luke Gross, our American second row, who found his bed in the corridor of the hotel. It was completely made, just as it would have been in his room, ready for him to sleep in!

There have always been some great characters in the dressing-room but my favourite battle was between Dwayne Peel and

Mark Jones, the current Scarlets captain. Peely and Boycey have been going hammer and tongs at each other for as long as I can remember and fight like cat and dog. They are always trying to get one over on each other. Before Peely left for Sale Sharks in the Guinness Premiership, they were a formidable double act and I loved throwing a hand grenade in between them every now and then, just to set them off. My favourite prank is the legendary 'sheepgate' incident during the 2007 World Cup in France.

We were staying in our base in La Baule, but it was, shall we say, a bit quiet and so the players found different ways to amuse themselves and each other. People were finding fruit or baked beans in their beds, but on this one occasion the situation escalated out of control. Boycey had found four bicycles in his room and was convinced Peely was the instigator. Boycey, who is the son of a farmer, had noticed there were some sheep in the grounds of the team hotel. It was like a red rag to a bull . . . or should that be sheep? I don't know. Anyway, he'd had enough and decided to really up the ante, so he picked up one of the sheep and walked into the hotel and locked it in Peely's room.

As if that wasn't enough, he then went back and picked up the ram of the herd and was walking back towards the hotel, followed by the rest of the sheep in the herd. It was only when he got to the entrance of the hotel that he was stopped by one of the staff and ordered to put the sheep down. The mess that one sheep made in Peely's room was enough, though. The sheep had gone through all of Peely's stuff and relieved itself all over his room. The smell was terrible – and Peely had to stay in that room for two weeks! Brilliant.

My first real introduction to the world of professional rugby was training with Frano Botica at Stradey. Frano was a former All Black and had returned to rugby union after a very successful stint with the Wigan rugby league side. I used to train with Frano and would kick the balls back to him during his kicking sessions and just hang around him, trying to pick up any tips I could. I am sure he must have thought I was a right pest, but he was patient and put up with a Welsh kid who wanted to help him out. I was just a young pup keen to learn as much as I could. Frano was one of the best goal-kickers around and I have always believed the ideal way to improve is to learn from the best. So that is what I did.

We soon came to an agreement that whoever landed the final drop goal during these sessions would have lunch bought for him. I won the first competition and he took me out and bought me a baguette and a drink. The following week Frano won so I took him out, but he stung me for steak and chips in a restaurant. He had a starter, main course and dessert! I learnt my lesson after that.

Although the game had gone professional, there were no organised weights sessions or anything like that, but Frano, Garan Evans, Sean Gale and I formed our own training group. We would meet most mornings in the old weights room under the stand in Stradey and do a weights session for an hour.

The early years of professional rugby in Wales were a real struggle, with every club making mistakes along the way. Llanelli were no different and in 1997 we hit a major financial problem. Stradey Park was leased back to the Welsh Rugby Union, as the club tried to stabilise itself. That was when Huw Evans, the current chairman, came on board and rescued the club. If he hadn't have done so when he did, the club would have disappeared and been another Bridgend or Pontypridd. Scarlets supporters and players have a lot to thank Huw for, because he kept professional rugby in the area. There is no way we would have competed in the Heineken Cup without his backing. He was committed to the Scarlets, fought for the Scarlets to be a regional side and is still fighting for the cause.

When the financial crisis hit the club back then, I was already happy with my £10,000 and club car, but all the players were told they were going to have to take around a 25 per cent pay cut to keep the club afloat. A new performance-related £500 win-bonus system was introduced, but it was a traumatic time for everybody at the club. I can remember all the players queuing up outside the club's main office, waiting to find out what their fate would be. One by one, they came out of the office in an absolute state of shock after discovering a quarter of their salary would be taken off them. I walked in fearing the worst, but walked out with a pay increase of £2,000 and was told I was on the new win-bonus system. I was one of the low earners at the club, but I still couldn't believe what had happened. I was the only one who walked out with a smile on his face.

The £500 win-bonus was massive at the time and a real incentive for the whole squad to make sure we won more games than we lost. When the club was in better financial shape, it would be reduced to £250 a win but, by then, all the players had had their basic salaries increased anyway. Llanelli weren't the only rugby side to struggle in the new professional era, but we survived it. Some clubs in Wales, England and France weren't so lucky and are now amateur, having been unable to retain their status in the top flight.

My coach for the whole of my first eight years at Stradey was Gareth Jenkins. We had a good relationship and much of the club's success was down to him. He was a hugely inspirational figure for Llanelli and later the Scarlets. He was part of the Llanelli side that beat the All Blacks in 1972 – probably the greatest day in our history – and understands the tradition of the place. Nobody should underestimate what he has done for the side. Without him, I doubt whether we would have reached two Heineken Cup semi-finals, in 2000 and 2002. His pre-match talks, which have gone down in folklore, would just drip with emotion. He knew what Llanelli and the Scarlets meant to the people of the town, the area and the region, and he could break it down so you knew you were playing for real people and for a team with a unique history, and that we all had a responsibility to lay our bodies on the line for the cause. He would ram home how we were the chosen ones and were so lucky to represent the people who had paid to come and watch us. Gareth's ability to motivate a Scarlet player was a gift. Even now, when I see him and speak to him, he has a way of talking about the side that is spine-tingling; it just gets under my skin.

I wouldn't do him justice by merely telling you what he used to say in the dressing-room before a game, but my favourite example of his ability to motivate his players occurred before we played Gloucester at Kingsholm in the Heineken Cup in 2001. Gareth had really wound us up a couple of hours before kick-off in a meeting at the team hotel. All the players were in the zone as we got on the team coach and headed to the ground. Nobody said a word when we got to Kingsholm and we were preparing ourselves to walk off the bus to the dressing-room when Gareth stood up at the front and said, 'Hit it, driver! Hit it!' The Welsh national anthem came blaring out of the loudspeakers and he was singing and punching the air in front of us. There we were, an hour and a half before kick-off with the Gloucester supporters walking around our bus with our anthem blaring out of the speakers. Incredible. The boys were ready to go to war when we finally got on the pitch. We started the game on such an emotional high. I have never been so pumped up for a rugby game in my life.

We played really well in that game but still lost in the dying moments to an Elton Moncrieff drop goal, which hit the back of our prop, Phil Booth, and went over. We lost 28–27 and were out of Europe. Peter Herbert, our fitness coach, copped much of the flak for months for that defeat. Herby, you see, had managed the impossible by getting Boothy fit enough to be somewhere on the pitch he would never normally have been.

That Llanelli side should have won the Heineken Cup. We came close, in semi-finals against Northampton Saints and the Leicester Tigers, but never reached a final. I believe we were certainly good enough to win the tournament because we had a really strong side, full of good players and good characters. Scott Quinnell was at his peak then and was a world-class player for us. He was brilliant and is an awesome man. He led the charge and we all followed him, but I am sure SQ would be the first to admit most of our success back then was down to Gareth. He was a superb man-manager, kept the players happy and looked after some big characters, some big egos, and got the best out of us. Welsh rugby still hadn't got to grips with professionalism, but Llanelli kept reaching the quarter-finals and semi-finals of Europe. We were – and I know this has become a bit of a cliché – Welsh rugby's flagbearers in the Heineken Cup.

That is why we were so successful in the Welsh Cup for so long. I can remember when Swansea beat us in the Cup final at Ninian Park in 1999 by 37–10. Scott Gibbs claimed it had been 'men against boys' after they had beaten us and lifted the trophy, but we remembered it and beat them in the final the following season. Gareth didn't have to remind us about Gibbsy's remarks – we were the kind of side that latched onto instances such as this to motivate ourselves.

The Scarlets are a very unique side, with a set of core values. The club not only promotes a certain insularity but also an openness to outside influences; it is a strange mix, but because of it European rugby held no fears for us. We were always a pretty cosmopolitan side and I think being in West Wales, so far away from everybody else, created a unique mindset. We never feared anybody back then and would just concentrate on what we wanted to do in any given game. I can remember Martin Johnson, Lawrence Dallaglio and even somebody such as Paul O'Connell telling me that travelling to play Llanelli at Stradey Park was always a daunting prospect. Back then, we were beating English club sides when Wales couldn't get anywhere near England at international level. I can remember in the 2001–02 season beating Leicester convincingly, a side which had six of the English pack at the time. We only lost by three points in the return game at Welford Road. They hadn't lost at home for something like 40 games on the bounce, and we lost by just 12–9 to them, and should have beaten them on their home patch. We would lose to the Tigers in the semi-final at the City Ground in Nottingham at the end of that same season. That was probably the one season when we were good enough to win the Heineken Cup. It was the closest we would come to lifting that trophy, and it has still eluded us.

I don't know how he did it, but Gareth just instilled a self-belief; we didn't care who we played, because we always believed we would win. We played sides with bigger budgets and bigger squads, but were always competitive. We were even the first Welsh side to win on French soil in the Heineken Cup in 2000, when we beat Bourgoin. Stuart Gallacher, our chief executive, got so excited when he knew we were on the brink of a historic victory that he got shown a yellow card by the referee for straying outside the technical area on the pitch. There is no doubt that we set the standard for Welsh sides in the Heineken Cup, and that is something I am still very proud of. Llanelli, a small town in West Wales, were a side to be feared and a major force in European rugby.

But the European Cup run that I enjoyed the most came much later, with the Scarlets in the 2007 season. Gareth had left to coach Wales, and Phil Davies, another former Scarlet, succeeded him at Stradey. Phil's appointment was all about the boot-room mentality, similar to that of the great Liverpool FC during the '60s, '70s and '80s. Gareth, Phil and Nigel Davies, our current coach, have all played for the side and instinctively understand what it means to be a Scarlet. Phil made a lot of changes when he came in. He was a very modern coach and very different from Gareth, but he knew when to pull at your heartstrings and could get very emotional about the side, too. He would get the likes of Phil Bennett, Derek Quinnell, Ray Gravell and Jonathan Davies, all Scarlets legends, to hand out our jerseys and talk to us before a game. To hear players of that calibre speak about how honoured they were to pull on the Scarlets jersey and what it meant to them was humbling and inspiring. It made you so proud to be following in their footsteps, and put the history and tradition of the side into context. Hearing legends of the world game like that remember the great games they had played for the side was just incredible

– it made you want to put your body on the line for the cause.

Phil had come up with a game plan for his first season in charge and it showed what a clever coach he was. He knew we weren't a big physical side, so we were to be a running side. We played that way, and it worked. We didn't train to win the battle at the contact area, but to be a running team. We were a physically light side but were skilful and wanted to move the ball at every opportunity. The style was perfect for the side, and we were encouraged to express ourselves on the field. We played in the number 13 channel and when you have a talent like Regan King on your side, it is obvious you have to get the ball in his hands at every opportunity. As we weren't physically a big side, playing in that area meant we were playing away from the opposition's forwards, where it was less congested and we wouldn't be bullied at the breakdown. Phil, whenever he talked in a team meeting, would always say, 'Expression, Regan.' Some of the boys thought those two words followed each other in the dictionary, they were used so often. Phil, though, wanted us to back ourselves and play rugby because we were a talented running side.

That side's best performance was probably the Scarlets' greatest victory away from home in the Heineken Cup. The way we beat Toulouse, the Real Madrid of European rugby, at home, in 2006, was fantastic, but we had to show some real resilience in the first half. When we had the ball, we were pretty decent, but they weren't bad either and quickly built a big lead. Dafydd James had scored a crucial try just before half-time to keep us in the game and we were on fire in the second half. We played some great rugby and matched them in every aspect when we had the ball. The week before the game, Rob Jones, our skills coach, had suggested that I fake kick a drop goal and then run. I did exactly that right at the end of the game. As I went back into the pocket and shaped for a drop goal, I heard Regan shout to me, 'Let's go, Steve!' I turned round and passed him the ball and he danced around three or four Toulouse defenders and Nathan Thomas scored the final try of the game to get us a 41–34 victory. Unbelievable. We had just done something we had spoken about earlier in the week and it had come off against probably the best side in Europe. We were a side now full of confidence and would win all our Pool games in Europe. We would beat Munster in the quarter-finals on a great European night at Stradey before being knocked out by Leicester in the semi-finals for a second time.

The following season was very different. It finished with Phil losing his job. We didn't win a game in our Heineken Cup Pool, but there were reasons for what happened to the side. So many of the senior players at the Scarlets were on World Cup duty at the start of Phil's second season in charge. Dwayne Peel, Matthew Rees, Mark Jones, Dafydd James and I were with Wales, while Simon Easterby was with Ireland, so there were hardly any senior players around to steady the ship, and we were all Phil's link to the rest of the squad. He used his senior players to bounce ideas off and to get his message across.

Phil looked after me. He didn't play me in every game, didn't burn me out and it was the freshest I have ever felt during my career. He was always on the phone, talking about moves and new ideas for training. Phil was professional, worked hard and was committed to the Scarlets cause and wanted us to improve. He was a Scarlet through and through. What happened to him was very messy. He deserved better. We didn't build on the success of his first season in charge and most of the signings from that second season have now left the Scarlets.

I am sure there are plenty of people who have enjoyed our downfall in recent years (because we were so successful in the Welsh Cup and were the inaugural winners of the Celtic League) and wonder how we were ever successful. What the Scarlets need now is continuity. All the successful sides have a nucleus of players who have been together for a while and have come through the tough times together. Just look at Wales.

The saddest part for me is that when you look at team photos from over the last four years it shows the number of players who have come and gone from the squad. It never used to be like that. We were always a settled side, with a core of players in the squad, and we would build around them. New players take a while to buy into what you are doing and have to learn and understand what it means to pull on the Scarlets jersey. It takes a number of years to build a team and you need time to let the dust settle. I know we have had to make some tough decisions for financial reasons, but it hasn't helped the continuity of the squad. We have to learn the lessons from the way we lost Dafydd James and Gavin Thomas because of an injury clause in their contracts. I felt for both of them – there were no winners in that situation.

I hope last season was a watershed for us. Things aren't going to happen or change overnight and everybody needs to be patient as we try to re-establish ourselves. We have a new stadium, Parc y Scarlets, and have to create a new history there. Nobody loved Stradey Park more than me, and the last game there was a very emotional evening. It was my second home, but we have to move on.

The Scarlets have a unique philosophy, and a history and tradition you just cannot buy, but there are things we have to take a long, hard look at. For example, apart from the great Quinnell family dynasty, we don't have a great record of producing international forwards from our region. Players such as Jonathan Thomas, Mefin Davies, Luke Charteris and Deiniol Jones, who have played for Wales, are all from the region but have never worn a Scarlets jersey. I think Dafydd Jones was the last born-and-bred Scarlet forward to play for Wales, and he made his international debut in 2002. The Scarlets side that beat Toulouse at home in France in the Heineken Cup had five threequarters from the region and five Welsh players in the pack. Mike Phillips, Lee Byrne and Andy Powell, who are now key players for Wales and were on the 2009 Lions tour, are all former Scarlets but have left the region. Signing players who are right for the region, not just good players, can take a side forward dramatically. I am not sure if we have really appreciated that. These are all issues we have to understand and address if we are going to get back to where we belong.

The Scarlets have been through some tough times, but we have always pulled together and pulled through. I have been there when we have done that. We are a side and an organisation in transition at the moment, there is no doubt about that. We are way off where we should be and everybody, inside and outside the club, recognises that. The supporters, I hope, understand that too. I never take the Scarlets fans for granted, because I know how expensive it is to follow the team around Europe. I will never forget what they went through to see us beat Bath in the 2002 Heineken Cup quarter-final at the Recreation Ground. The game was postponed due to a waterlogged pitch and the fans drove up the M4 and then returned 24 hours later to support us the next day. Not many sets of supporters would do that when they know the game is also on TV.

I do hope there is a new realism about our ambitions and what we have to do to get back to where we were, particularly in Europe. Only the likes of Munster, Leicester, Toulouse and London Wasps have a better record in the Heineken Cup, but the difference is those sides have all won the tournament. We haven't – but that still has to be our long-term goal. The Scarlets have to evolve.

The one organisation we have to look at is Munster. We are both very similar, but Munster probably learnt the lessons of their failures better than we did. They, like the Scarlets, are a pretty insular organisation, but they have made that a real strength, not a weakness. I remember when they won the Heineken Cup; they had a side with 13 players from the province in the starting line-up. The Scarlets have to follow that model. I passionately believe that we need a nucleus of home-grown Scarlets at the core of the side, with a smattering of genuine world-class players to give us the experience and hard-nosed edge at the very highest level. We have some great young Scarlets, such as Jonathan Davies, Daniel Evans, Rhys Priestland, Lou Reed, Dominic Day, Ken Owens and

Aaron Shingler, to name but a few, in the current squad. They are real talents with great potential, but they also have a great work ethic. They are players you can build a squad around.

I know we face a big challenge; we have to be realistic about where the Scarlets are now. I know we have a great record in Europe and have had some great teams who have come so close to winning the Heineken Cup, but we did punch above our weight. It's time to focus on what we are doing and what we have and not worry about what we don't have. I was born in the region and for me it will always be the best region to play for in Wales. The people are passionate about the side and everybody has an opinion on the team – who should be in it and the style of rugby we should play. Not many places have that feeling for their rugby team. We have tradition, history and culture in abundance and are spoilt because we have all of that to draw on. Look at the players who have worn the number 10 jersey: Carwyn James, Barry John, Phil Bennett and Jonathan Davies. Which other rugby side can claim that?

I am very conscious of the legacy we have been left and we have to embrace it and build on it. The Scarlets are a rugby brand known around the rugby world. Rugby people in England, France, South Africa, New Zealand and Australia know who we are. How many other rugby sides can say that? We need to remind ourselves about things like that and get the unique values we have across to people. The bottom line is that we have to get back to where we were. The supporters deserve that and the history of the Scarlets demands that.

CHAPTER 4

VIVE LA FRANCE

Make it work!

– Gareth Jenkins, Scarlets and Wales coach

My back is killing me. I am flying back to France after being summoned to Cardiff by Andrew Hore, the Wales conditioning coach, for a fitness test that was a waste of time because I wasn't fit enough to even do it. I have been travelling for twenty-four hours and now, five flights later, via Amsterdam, Biarritz and Cardiff, I am flying back to Clermont.

I had been knocked unconscious on my debut by a cheap shot, a cynical elbow to my face. My new club had sacked their coach after only three games in charge and there I was, sitting in my seat with one phrase going through my mind: 'What have you done, Steve? What are you doing playing rugby in France?'

The air hostess comes over. She can see I am lost in my own little world and preoccupied. I order a bottle of red wine for the journey home. She has no idea who I am, but I am the fool who left the comfort of a rugby team I knew like the back of my hand, and my family and friends, because I wanted to try something new. I was the Wales fly-half and I am so far out of my comfort zone it is frightening. I cannot speak the language. I got lost for two hours on my first day after I picked up my car only a couple of miles from my new home.

I could have signed for the Leicester Tigers, one of the biggest club sides in Europe, who had won the Heineken Cup twice, but I chose to come to France. Leicester had even offered me a better deal than the one I had signed to play in France but, of course, I knew what I was doing.

What the hell was I thinking?

This was a bad idea. What was I doing in France?

Anybody who knows me knows I am a pretty positive type of guy, but those first few weeks in France were the toughest of my rugby career. I was lonely. One man's words kept popping into my head during that time and to me they were prophetic. After I had told him I was off to play rugby in France, Gareth Jenkins, the Scarlets coach, had wished me well, but his parting words were, 'Steve, make it work.'

Throughout my career, I have never been one to shirk a challenge and Gareth's advice remained with me throughout my two years in France. Whenever I felt I'd had enough or things weren't going my way, I would remember what he had said to me, stop feeling sorry for myself, pull myself together and dig in. I had made the decision to come to France and I was the one who had to make it work.

I had done eight years with the Scarlets, and unlike most of my friends I had never lived or worked outside Wales. I had always been fascinated by French rugby, mainly because of my experiences with the Scarlets in the Heineken Cup. It was always a riot of noise and colour whenever I played there and rugby in France had really captured my imagination. The bands, the flags and the flares made playing in France such a unique experience.

There was a beauty and brutality about French rugby. In some ways, there was almost a split personality in their approach to the game: they could be unbelievably powerful and physical, but also play with such skill and flair, and I really wanted to know what made them so good.

I had come back from the 2003 World Cup and had made the decision in my mind to try something new outside Wales. Some feelers were put out to see if any clubs would be interested in signing me, and Leicester Tigers and Montferrand made it pretty clear they would like to talk to me.

During the 2004 Six Nations campaign, I had a decision to make about whether I wanted to play rugby in England or France. I had been mulling over the options for a while: Leicester, a real super-power in Europe, had won the Heineken Cup twice; Montferrand, meanwhile, were an unknown quantity with a reputation as under-achievers in the French championship.

Gareth was brilliant with me. I had been open and honest with the club and told them that I was thinking of leaving at the end of that season. They made it very clear they wanted me to stay and put an offer on the table, but I had pretty much made the decision I was leaving and it was just a case of where I would be going. Gareth had been as good as gold and told me to take some time off to mull over my options. I went to Leicester to see the set-up, meet the coaches and get a feel for what they were about as a team.

But my visit to Leicester really was a comedy of errors from start to finish. Any hope I had of keeping a possible move to the Midlands under wraps proved impossible. I drove up to Leicester to meet Peter Wheeler, the chief executive, in a hotel and when I walked into the foyer, all the Glamorgan cricket team were there. I couldn't believe it! I told Peter we should probably find a different hotel, but all I could hear as we walked out were the Glamorgan boys shouting, 'Don't sign! Stay in Wales!'

The Tigers really looked after me on my trip up there. Peter had organised for the likes of Geordan Murphy, their Irish international, and Lewis Moody, the England World Cup winner, to take me out to dinner that evening. I had got to know the pair of them both pretty well over the years and it was great to catch up with them and get a feel for the club from their point of view. There were about half a dozen of us and it turned out to be a very good, but very long, night. We had a few beers, then a few more, then a few more, and ended up in some nightclub in the early hours. I returned to my hotel completely smashed. It had been a great night, but I was in a disgraceful state for a professional rugby player.

I was woken up by an alarm call in my hotel room, sprawled across my bed, in the same clothes I had worn the night before, and in an absolute mess. I spent half an hour in a cold shower trying to sober up before I met John Wells and the rest of the Leicester coaching and management team. Peter picked me up at 8 a.m. and only then did I discover that the Leicester players had been given the day off. Thanks, boys! It was a pretty special welcome to the Tigers.

I spent two hours with the Leicester coaches, talking about their plans and what they wanted from me, but to this day I am ashamed to say I cannot remember a thing about it. I don't remember what I said or what was said to me. It's all a complete blank.

A few hours later I had sobered up and drove the three hours back home. I couldn't believe what I had done. I thought I had just blown a golden opportunity to play for one of the biggest sides in Europe. I was convinced they wouldn't want me after my behaviour, but thankfully they made it very clear they were still happy to sign me.

The next few weeks were tough. All the self-doubts started to surface about whether I should move. I was leaving somewhere I knew like the back of my hand – I knew the groundsman and even the name of his dog – for something unknown. I knew I wanted the challenge of a completely new experience, but the Scarlets were firing on all cylinders – they would go on to win the inaugural Celtic

League title. The place was my home and where my family and all my friends were. We had a cracking team, some real strength-in-depth, with the likes of Dwayne Peel and Mike Phillips, two brilliant scrum-halfs, battling it out for the number 9 jersey.

There were many sleepless nights and endless pros and cons lists drawn up, as I mulled over the three offers on the table. The best financial package was from the Tigers, followed by Montferrand and then the Scarlets, but the reason for the move wasn't about money. It was about getting out of my comfort zone. I was single at the time and had no real commitments, and it just seemed the perfect time to see a bit of the world. Professional rugby does offer you the chance to play in different countries and when those opportunities come, you'd be a fool not to consider them.

The whole situation was complicated even further by the fact that Pat Howard, the former Wallabies centre, was leaving Montferrand to return to Leicester as coach and he was talking to me about signing for the Tigers. He would be on the phone from France, saying Clermont wasn't the place for me and that I should sign for Leicester. It was a bizarre time, to say the least.

After weighing up all the options, I decided I wanted something completely different and decided to sign for Montferrand. I later found out that there was some rubbish doing the rounds that Scott Johnson had turned my head and told me to go to France and leave the Scarlets. That was nonsense; it was my decision and mine alone. In fact, Johno would probably have preferred it if I had stayed in Wales because it would have been much easier for the national set-up to keep an eye on me.

My decision to sign for Montferrand wasn't helped by a telephone conversation I had with Tony Marsh. I had rung him to get a feel for the club and he told me, in a typically blunt Kiwi way: 'Listen, mate. The club isn't doing that well. I wouldn't sign if I were you.' When I met up with him for the first time after I had signed, he turned to me and said, 'I don't know why I bothered talking to you, you didn't listen to a word I said!' It broke the ice between us straight away and was the beginning of a good friendship. By then, I had moved into Pat's old flat after he had headed off to the Midlands. It had all been very surreal.

People said to me at the time that I was some kind of trailblazer because I was the first Welsh player to be tempted to France by a big-money move, but I never really saw it like that. It was just a chance to taste a new culture and become a better rugby player. I was confident that playing rugby in France would improve my skills. They had French coaches, too, which was great. I didn't see any point going to a side coached by a New Zealander or an Australian; I wanted to learn all about the French approach to the game, especially when it came to their attacking strategy.

Montferrand, though, would be a complete culture shock and so different from what I was used to at Stradey. At the first team meeting, the president of the club announced the team was changing its name to Clermont Auvergne. Friends would ring me up asking why I wasn't playing and if Montferrand had been relegated or even gone out of business.

The club had a reputation for being a bit of a railway station, with players coming and going every year. They liked to buy new players every season and had earned themselves a reputation for always looking for a quick-fix by signing this or that player. I had done my research on the club and knew its reputation within the rest of Europe. I went into the whole thing with my eyes wide open. The rugby club was supported by Michelin, but it didn't come close to having the financial support that the company gave Formula One. They had a fantastic following and the rugby club was a gift to the town by the company for its employees. The place had strong working-class roots and reminded me so much of Llanelli. The rugby team was very important to the supporters, but after a game the fans could switch off, whether the team had won or lost.

I arrived a week before pre-season and it took me a while to get my bearings. Like I said, when I picked up my car it took me two hours to get home because I got lost. I didn't know the language and had never driven on the right-hand side of the road before. I was scared to use my car for the first couple of weeks because I was afraid of getting lost again, so I walked most places around town.

My first day in training wasn't any better. The three French internationals I knew – Aurélien Rougerie, Tony Marsh and Olivier Magne – had been given an extra week off because they had been on a summer tour with France. So there I was in a new club, a new dressing-room, and I didn't know anybody. But the players were brilliant to me. Every one of them came up and shook my hand and made me feel very welcome . . . but I couldn't help thinking about what the boys would be doing back at the Scarlets. Everybody at Montferrand made a real effort to make me feel at home. For the first month, I was taken out nearly every night for dinner in a restaurant or invited to someone's home, as I made the transition to the French way of life.

On the field, the pressure was on. I was the big signing and was there to fight with Gérald Merceron, the club's French international, for the number 10 shirt. He is a great player but had lost confidence in his kicking and that was why I had been signed. My first game was a real introduction to French rugby. We were playing against Montpellier, and I launched a bomb skywards, set off after it and was floored by a cheap shot by their scrum-half. He elbowed me in the face and I had to be carried off the field in a hell of a state. All I can remember is being in the dugout, looking down at my shirt and thinking, Why am I wearing a blue jersey – I usually wear a red shirt? I was completely out of it. Apparently, I had a conversation with Gregor Townsend, the former Scotland fly-half, after the game, but I cannot remember a thing about it. I had just had my first taste of the physical and uncompromising nature of the game in France.

Anything and everything goes in France, even in training. The Argentinian boys at Clermont had no qualms about dragging their fingers across your face in a mock attempt to eye-gouge you. They would do it with a smile on their faces and laugh about it, but it was almost like a warning about what to expect and to look after yourself on the field. French rugby is unrelentingly brutal and there is a lot that goes on on the pitch. It's not as violent as it used to be in the '70s and '80s: listening to the stories of what the game was like back then, I was astonished. What I will say is that a red card in the Magners League or the Guinness Premiership would probably only get you a yellow card in the Top 14 in France.

But I loved playing in France, even if it was a real culture shock. The grounds were always packed, bands would be playing and the stands were always full when you ran out for your pre-match warm-up. Every game was just a real event. Welsh rugby could learn a lot from French rugby about how to sell the game to the paying customer.

Neil McIlroy, the Clermont team manager, was a Scotsman from the Borders who had found himself in France, and he was a great confidant and help to me. He met me at the airport when I first arrived for pre-season, invited me to his home for dinner and then he took me to the apartment that would become home. Neil was fantastic to me and looked after me throughout my two-year spell there.

He loves telling anybody who will listen about an interview I did with a French journalist in Clermont after Wales had won the Grand Slam in 2005. He sat in on the interview to make sure nothing was lost in translation between the journalist and myself. I was trying to speak in pidgin French and he was doing the same in English. He asked me how 'historic' the Grand Slam was for Wales, but I thought he had started talking about 'Easter eggs'. Don't ask! I was bemused and replied that we hadn't eaten any Easter eggs. We were both looking at each other, utterly confused.

Meanwhile, Neil was doubled-up, roaring with laughter at the two of us failing miserably to communicate. I didn't do many interviews with French journalists after that! How historic became Easter eggs, I will never know.

But nobody worked as hard or had the players' or the club's interests at heart like Neil. When I see the success Clermont are having now, I always think about Neil and how much he must be enjoying it – and he deserves it.

After the celebrations of winning the Grand Slam with Wales, Clermont had been good enough to give me the week off when I returned to the club. I made sure that I let all the Welsh boys who were back on Celtic League duty know that I had been given some time off by sending a text to them.

The most enjoyable weekend of my whole time in France was after we had beaten Les Blues at the Stade de France on the way to winning the Grand Slam. I had arranged to meet Pierre Mignoni and Aurélien Rougerie at the French team's hotel to get a lift back to Clermont. I turned up with a big smile on my face because I had won the man of the match award for the game, but I didn't say a word. I just got into the car, sat down and burst out laughing. There was an uncomfortable silence, then just the sound of me laughing. I don't think they enjoyed the journey, but I certainly did. I couldn't keep the smile off my face and took the piss out of them all the way back home. It was a great journey for a Welshman in France!

The Clermont squad did have some great characters and we spent quite a bit of time together, going for meals or coffee, and sitting down for a long lunch, as is part of the French culture. For a squad with players from all over the world, we were a pretty tight group. The players would sit down for a two-hour lunch together at the club's superb canteen and it was a real social occasion. In fact, my new-found love of food stems from my time in France; before that I was a classic Brit and saw food as just a refuelling exercise. I would grab a meal before rushing out here or there – it was something I did, rather than enjoyed. I can remember some of the boys coming over to my apartment just after I had arrived and checking out my fridge and finding a quiche and a tomato. Not a great impression to make when you are in one of the culinary centres of the world!

My appreciation of food changed while I was in France because we had players from different regions in France and from around the world. We would discuss food, wine, cheese and our favourite local dishes. It would all get very competitive. We would think nothing of heading out to a local restaurant or bistro to eat. Even the French supermarkets were an absolute eye-opener for a guy from Carmarthen. The selection of foods available, like live lobster and crab, just blew me away.

Food is a real focal point in French life, and I loved it. Players would invite me around to their homes for meals and, for me, it just added to the whole experience of life there. Gonzalo Longo, the Clermont and Argentina number 8, invited me to his home and his wife cooked a superb Argentinian meal for me. All the Argentinian boys were brilliant with me; they looked after me and had a great outlook on life. They were very intelligent and gracious people and would shake my hand every day before we trained. It would become a daily ritual in the dressing-room to shake the hands of every member of the squad, so I always tried to get in early for training to make sure I didn't have to be the one going around shaking everybody's hands.

One of the real characters was Olivier Saisset, the forwards coach, who had played for Béziers in the '80s when they had won five French Championships. He was an old-school forwards coach and a really hard taskmaster, and was feared by the whole squad. He was also a chain-smoker and always had a cigarette in his mouth. You could always tell when he was coming because a cloud of smoke would arrive before he did.

Then there was Aurélien Rougerie, the French international

wing, who is the best athlete I have ever played alongside. And Mario Ledesma, the Argentina hooker, one of the best players in the world. He is shaped like a pear. I used to look at him and think, How can you be a rugby player? But what a rugby brain and player he was! There was Marc Renaud, one of our French forwards, who was your quintessential Frenchman and would rarely speak English. I only found out he and a couple of the other French forwards spoke English when he replied in fluent English to one of my comments – a couple of months after I had arrived at the club! I had been struggling to make myself understood to quizzical looks from the guys up until then.

Then there was the legendary Sébastien Viars, who played full-back for us. He epitomised what I would call French flair. He was an amazing counter-attacking full-back. He could do everything with the ball in his hands, he was a fantastic runner and he could kick. He was an amazing talent, but a unique character. I can remember asking him how many times he had played for France. 'Not enough,' he replied. Brilliant.

Seb hated tackling and hated playing on a muddy pitch. I can remember we played against Lyonnaise away from home and their pitch was like a mudbath. We all came off caked in the stuff, apart from Seb. He came over to me in a clean kit and said, 'Steve, look at me. I am beautiful. I didn't make one tackle.'

I was the unknowing victim of Seb's aversion to tackling once when we played Grenoble. They were on the attack and had this massive forward lined up to carry the ball down Seb's defensive channel, but he managed to shuffle out of the way and left me to deal with the monster charging right at me. The Grenoble forward bowled me over as if I wasn't there; he went straight over the top of me. We watched a video of the game in the debrief the following week and Seb piped up, 'Look at this, everybody. Steve is getting killed.' He was great value, one of the great characters of that Clermont side and a brilliant bloke.

But my time in France wasn't without its bizarre moments. The start of my first season was a nightmare. The side couldn't get a win for love nor money. I can remember being told by our backs coach that an opposition winger always liked to come in looking for an interception pass. Then I unfortunately threw a pass and he did exactly that and raced in for a try. Not one of my finer moments. Then we played in Paris against Stade Français, who had a great squad and were one of the real powerhouses of French rugby, and lost a game we should have won. We were ahead and in control of the game, which had been pretty tasty, when one of our younger players completely lost it. We had a scrum and he just launched the ball at one of Stade Français players and hit him square in the face. We went on to lose the game and didn't even get a bonus point for our trouble, when we should have won it.

I can remember meeting Gareth Thomas for a coffee the night before we played Toulouse, whom he had signed for. It was the first time we were due to play each other on French soil. We compared notes and admitted we were lucky to be playing in probably the best domestic rugby competition in the world. There we were, two Welsh guys, one from Carmarthen and the other from Bridgend, about to play in one of the real glamour games of the French rugby calendar. I came out on top that night, but what an occasion, and what an event to be a part of.

I was voted best fly-half in the French Championship by rugby magazine *Midi Olympique* in my first season at Clermont. That was a huge honour, especially when the likes of Freddie Michalak, David Skrela and Manny Edmonds were all playing in the Championship, too. I was also named in the Lions squad to tour New Zealand that season. The Lions weren't really a big deal in France, but when Tony Marsh announced that I had been selected I got a round of applause from the whole of the Clermont squad, and that really meant a lot to me.

My second season in France was hard work. I returned from New

Zealand and went straight to work almost as soon as I returned. I didn't have a pre-season to speak of. I'd also had a niggling ankle injury for most of that campaign.

But I love French rugby and its many idiosyncrasies – that is what makes it so fascinating for me. This is a country renowned for its attacking flair, but the supporters love the driving maul and the grunt and grind of the forward battle. I can remember the Clermont pack driving from a lineout from the halfway line for a try, with me strolling behind them with my hands on my hips, and the crowd just going ballistic. I guess there can be beauty in the ugliest of things sometimes, and that is what makes rugby such a compelling game.

Rugby in France did open my eyes to the cut-throat and ruthless nature of professional sport. In Wales, if you were released by a region, you could get another contract with another region and still live in the same place and keep the kids in the same school. In France, players were really playing for their contract, livelihood and the future of their families. I can remember my final season when we played Bayonne, who were bottom in the league. We needed to win to qualify for Europe and they needed to win to stay in the league. The game was absolutely brutal because we were up against players who were fighting for their financial survival. It hammered home to me what professional sport is all about – winning is everything when your family's future is at stake.

It brought home to me that my job was to play rugby – it is what I got paid to do. I had never really felt that way in Wales. I had been very sheltered back home and had everything laid on a plate for me. I was one of the chosen ones, being a Welsh international; there were so many people there to look after me and to make sure I had the best of everything. Even while I was in France, Caroline Morgan, the team secretary, always arranged everything for me when I returned to Wales for squad training or for the Autumn Test series and the Six Nations.

I took a lot from my time in France. It made me more confident.

I learnt to look after myself. When I became the first Clermont player to win the prestigious Top 14 player of the month award for a couple of seasons, I even managed to deliver my acceptance speech in French to about 200 people, in front of my teammates. I would never have dreamt I would have done something like that when I had first arrived in France. My experiences there have a big effect on how I deal with any players who come to the Scarlets from overseas. In the past, I would have trained, played and gone home to my family and friends. Now, when a new player arrives, I always make a point of welcoming him and taking him out for a meal or something, and checking he is OK and not being left on his own all the time. Some players arrive, like I did in Clermont, completely on their own and are trying to settle into a new country, a new home and a new side, and they just need some help to find their feet. Gareth Jenkins has always been really good at doing that at the Scarlets, but I like to do the same now. The Clermont players invited me to join them for dinner or lunch, when I couldn't speak a word of French and couldn't take part in any of their conversations, and I really feel they looked after me. There is no reason I cannot do the same for any new faces at the Scarlets.

Moving to Clermont had been exactly what I needed and it pushed me out of my comfort zone. When I left, the club even organised a surprise party for me and presented me with a Clermont shirt signed by everybody connected with the club. The Georgians had even written something in Georgian. To this day, I still don't know what it says. Clermont had made it pretty clear they wanted me to stay for a third season, but I told them that I wanted to return to Wales, basically to prepare for the 2007 World Cup. They had been fantastic to me. They could have made life very difficult and not even played me for the remaining part of the season, but they didn't. They respected my decision and gave me time to arrange my return home. At the end of my two years in France, I jumped in my car with a couple of mates and we went on a great road trip through the middle of France before returning home to Wales. It was a great way to end a fantastic life and rugby experience.

My two years in France had a massive impact on me. I was now a better rugby player and a better person. The whole experience opened my mind to new experiences and got me to appreciate different cultures and people from different backgrounds. Before I went there I had only known rugby with the Scarlets and believed the way we did things there was the right way to do things. Everything, from the way we trained and played to the lifestyle, was so different. It taught me that there isn't one right way to do things. Clermont were bloody good to me and I loved my time there. The French attitude to life was just spot on and I wouldn't have changed the experience for the world.

CHAPTER 5

THE DRESSING-ROOM

It's at the border of pain and suffering that the men are separated from the boys.

– Emil Zátopek, long-distance runner
and three-times Olympic gold medallist

The dressing-room is a sacred place. It's the one place I will probably miss more than any other when my career is over. It's where you see players and coaches at their best, at their most vulnerable and at their most raw. It's where you see someone's real character come to the fore. It's your workplace during the week, and then the best or worst of places after a game. Simply, there isn't a place quite like it.

Walking into a dressing-room before a big game and walking out after one are so different. When a team arrives for a match, the dressing-room is silent, pristine and spotless. Nobody says much and you can feel the tension, the drive and the ambition in the room. You can sense the anticipation and the nervous energy, and can even taste the fear. For some players, the build-up on the morning of a game before kick-off is a terrible pressure and they wonder why they put themselves through all the agony when all they want to do is play. Once the referee has blown to start the game, they are fine and are where they love to be. But, depending on whether we win or lose, that dressing-room can dictate my mood for days afterwards.

When somebody is under pressure, you see their true colours. You see the best and worst of people. Some change out of sight in the dressing-room and become very different characters. Those who are very confident and sure of themselves become very quiet and focused, while those players who are very quiet outside the dressing-room just seem to come to life.

Seeing players and coaches in that kind of high-pressure environment, you get to know them very well indeed. You see how people react to pressure and disappointment, and how they deal with success, but more importantly failure. The public image of a player can be very different from what they are like in a dressing-room. Sport, at the very top end, does reveal a person's true character. There is no hiding place. The higher you go up the ladder, the more exposed you are to your teammates and your coaches. You are there to be shot at and to be shot down by the thousands in the stands and the millions watching on TV.

We all have strengths and weaknesses, and it's up to the individual to use his or her strengths and improve those weaknesses. Some players and coaches come alive when their backs are against the wall and they have been written-off by everyone. Without breaking any dressing-room code or giving too much away, the Welsh public's perceptions are probably way off the mark when they imagine how some players are in the dressing-room. Some players, who may appear confident and really in control of themselves in public, are the complete opposite in private. They are motivated by self-doubt and the fear of failure. That fear of letting people down is probably the one thing that all sportsmen share.

Some players are a bag of nerves before a game. Neil Jenkins always used to throw up before a game, but then would be calmness personified in the heat of a Test match. Ryan Jones, the current Wales captain, is the same. Rupert Moon wouldn't shut up. He would always talk non-stop, but Moonie was like that every day of the week! Martyn Madden would be gossiping about the latest this or that and would wind somebody up by telling him Graham Henry was here to run the rule over him for Wales. Chris Wyatt, the Wales and Scarlets lock, would always light up a cigarette and start smoking in the changing room when he came back in after a game. He would be sitting there, with his feet up, completely at peace with himself and the world. Lee Byrne would be reading a book in his cubicle before a game, while Mefin Davies would always be the first changed and asking me if I was ready to go out for some kicking practice. Mef is one of the nicest blokes around. He played for Wales towards the end of his rugby career and always wanted to soak it all up and take it all in. The sooner he could get out on the pitch and revel in the whole atmosphere, the better.

Some players read some good-luck messages from family and friends, while others just get lost in their own thoughts. Will Greenwood, the England World Cup winner, left a note on my kit ahead of the third Test between the Lions and South Africa, which read: 'Good luck and enjoy it.' Things like that really do mean a lot to the players. I had got to know Will really well on the 2005 Lions tour to New Zealand and it meant a lot that he had taken the time out to do something like that. Here was a triple Lions tourist from 1997, 2001 and 2005 and a World Cup winner taking the time out to wish me well.

Simon Easterby, the former Scarlets captain, would always be deep in thought before a game, looking for the right words or phrase to say to his team before kick-off. Easters is probably the most intense player I have ever shared a dressing-room with. He has probably been the greatest Scarlet of the professional era. He doesn't say much, but when he talks, people listen. He is the most loyal Scarlet and the most positive, and his belief in the cause is unshakeable. Then he does what every captain has to do and leads by example on the pitch, putting his body where it hurts. You cannot ask for any more than that from a captain or a teammate.

I have only seen one coach really lose it in a dressing-room. We were on tour in Argentina and were losing to the Pumas in Buenos Aires in 1999. Graham Henry, who could be pretty aloof and distant sometimes, lost it at half-time because we were losing and nobody expected it. I can remember him kicking a load of water bottles to get his point across – it certainly had the impact he desired because the boys came back from behind to win the game and win the Test series against the Pumas. Graham was always pretty constant and didn't get carried away with victory or defeat, and that was the first time we had seen a different side to him.

Being a Scarlet, I have heard all the stories about Delme Thomas's rousing speech before Llanelli beat the All Blacks at Stradey Park in 1972. I would love to have been a fly on the wall in that dressing-room and to have heard what he said. Professional rugby has changed all of that, though. In the amateur era, the game was all about emotion, adrenaline and attitude. Those players were as committed as the professional players for the big games, but the difference is that we have to do it every week. The game has also evolved out of sight in the professional era. Teams and players are analysed like never before, and every side has a strategy and game plan. The devil is in the detail, not the emotion. Paying attention to the minutiae, and the technical and tactical aspects, wins you rugby matches. Preparation is now key to success: you cannot go out onto the pitch pumped up to the eyeballs and play like an idiot.

The walk into the Stradey dressing-room, especially for the big Heineken Cup games, was something I always looked forward to. Before the Magners League and the Anglo-Welsh Cup were introduced into the season, we didn't have a regular diet of games against the big Irish provinces or the English clubs. Playing against the likes of Munster, London Wasps and Leicester Tigers always got the blood pumping, and it was the same whenever we played a French club at home. Stradey just used to come alive and there was almost a crackle of excitement about the place when you walked into the dressing-room. You could also hear the supporters arrive at the ground, and the tension would just build before the team would run out for the game. As a Scarlets player, knowing you are using the same dressing-room as some of the true greats and legends of the game was just awe-inspiring. The sense of history and tradition was palpable, and so was the expectation that we would deliver the right result.

The average Welsh rugby dressing-room has changed out of sight. I have seen soap and a can of Brut swapped for hair gel, hair wax, moisturiser and fake tan. There is probably more fake tan in the Welsh dressing-room than there is in a bodybuilders' changing room! I know some of the Irish and English boys were shocked on the recent Lions tour to South Africa to see the personal grooming routines of some of the Welsh boys! Rugby has changed in that respect and is a much more glamorous game. It is now a commodity to be sold to broadcasters, advertisers and sponsors. Nearly everybody these days has their own iPod, with their own motivational music on it; the days of the big tapedeck in the middle of the room, booming out some tune before kick-off are long gone, though there will always be music blaring out of a beatbox after a victory. Since Shaun Edwards has been in Wales it has become a tradition to sing 'Saturday Night at the Movies' after a win. All the boys wondered what was going on when he first started singing the song, on his own, after the win over England at Twickenham in 2008. We would end up singing the song quite a bit that season – all us knew the words by the time we had beaten France at the Millennium Stadium to win the Grand Slam.

Dressing-rooms used to be pretty basic places, with a physio table and pegs to hang your clothes on, and a big kit bag. But now they are quite spacious, with the dreaded ice-bath, a table full of isotonic drinks and food and your own special changing cubicle. They are usually covered in flags, banners or motivational phrases designed to make it a special place and to remind you who you are representing when you take the field.

Personally, I have always believed it's a player's personal responsibility to motivate himself and to make sure he is at his physical and mental peak for every game. If you aren't, you shouldn't be there. If you rely on a captain or a coach to get you where you need to be to play for your country, or whoever, you need to ask why you are playing the game.

Steve Hansen was the first coach who really rammed home what the dressing-room meant and what it said about a team. Before then, it was just seen as somewhere we changed and prepared for a game. Steve made the dressing-room almost a symbol of what we were about as a team and as individual players, coaches and people. He made it a golden rule that what went on in the dressing-room stayed in the dressing-room, and that anybody who opened the dressing-room door to the public needed to have a long, hard look at themselves. That was something I believed in from my days at Stradey Park.

The senior players at Llanelli had always set the tone of a dressing-room and at the Scarlets I was very lucky to have big characters like Robin McBryde and Moonie to guide me early on in my career. Moonie, in particular, who was my half-back partner, was a real calming influence on me when I started out playing. He could see I would get too emotional before a game and would always try to relax me, by whistling a song or something, as we walked out to play.

But it was Steve who believed the dressing-room represented a team and its values. He would demand that we left it as we found it – clean and tidy. Players were told to clean up their own stall or sweep the floor and make sure that it was spotless, so nobody else had to clean up after us. It was a statement about us to our hosts, about who we were and what we were about. Steve made it clear it was another element to being a professional outfit on and off the field. He believed it showed what our collective values were and that it was central to the team ethic he was determined to build in the squad. He and Alan Phillips, the Wales team manager, would have no qualms about sweeping the floor or tidying the place, and all the boys bought into it.

It underlined what we were all about and it was that kind of detail that had a profound effect on the national set-up. It was a statement about our respect for each other and told us that everybody in the set-up was equal. He demanded there would be no egos in the Wales dressing-room. He also believed it said something about the Welsh team and the country and people we represented. I always liked the idea that, wherever we toured, the cleaners would walk into our dressing-room and be amazed by what they found. It said something about us and about being Welsh and what the Wales team stood for.

Steve always used to say things like that, which made all the difference to the side. I can remember thinking, how does sweeping the floor make us a better rugby team? But he was right, because it meant if we did more than was asked off the pitch, it would become second nature to do it on the pitch.

When Wales get to the Millennium Stadium, the dressing-room is almost like a sanctuary: a place to collect your thoughts and to run through the technical and tactical aspects of the game. It is, quite literally, the calm before the storm of Test match rugby. The coaches and the captain will have said what they want to say at the team hotel. I usually get changed quickly and run out straight away and go through my ritual of 25 minutes of kicking to make sure I get my bearings on the field.

The captain will then say a few sentences and the coaches may say a few things to individual players, but it really is a place to collect your thoughts. International players don't have to be motivated to play; the days of mindless screaming and shouting are over. Stirring professional players into mindless banshees just doesn't work. For me, keeping my focus on the job I have to do and not getting wrapped up in the emotion of the occasion or who we are playing has been the biggest challenge. There have been times when the red mist has descended and I have just been too emotional running onto a rugby pitch, and that has clouded my judgement. It has meant that I haven't performed well or come close to doing my job for the team.

After a game, the atmosphere in a dressing-room can either be the best place in the world or like a morgue. The emotion really can go from one end of the spectrum to the other – there simply is no middle ground. That, too, has been something I have learned to handle over the years. Players and coaches have to find a middle ground and you cannot allow yourself to get carried away with success or failure. If you did, you would be an emotional basketcase and a physical wreck. But the silence in a dressing-room when you have lost is deafening. Players and coaches are usually completely lost in their own thoughts, trying to make sense of what has just happened. The coach or captain may say a few words, but they never really register because you have just failed to do what you set out to do. Every player has his own way of coping with defeat. I just try to deal with the negative emotions there and then, and move on.

One of the most desolate changing rooms I have ever been a part of – and felt most responsible for – was after Llanelli's 2002 Heineken Cup semi-final defeat to Leicester in Nottingham in 2002. I would quite happily burn every copy of the video or DVD of that game. I never want to watch it. I didn't enjoy that game at all, or the dressing-room afterwards. Knowing what I now know about the game, I would love to play that game again. I am pretty sure we would win it. Everybody knows about Tim Stimpson's penalty kick, which clinched victory for the Tigers, but I still felt there was so much, individually, that I could have done to win that game. I had a mixed game, kicking well, but my game-management was poor.

It was probably the lowest point of my career until being beaten by England in the warm-up games before the 2003 World Cup in Australia. I took both of those defeats very personally and they still live with me now.

But walking into a dressing-room when you have won a game is probably the biggest high you can have as a player. The feeling of accomplishment and achievement and the collective camaraderie is brilliant. You have just seen your best-laid plans succeed. It's like a drug, and you want more and more of it. I have been lucky enough to win two Grand Slams and the joy of seeing all your hard work and sacrifice actually being rewarded is incredible.

Seeing what it means to the supporters always surprises me. I know that if Wales win, then everybody goes to work for the next few days with an extra spring in their step. That is a huge responsibility to carry around, but is also something I have learned to embrace. Seeing the supporters delirious after the victory over Ireland in Cardiff in 2005 is something which will live long in my memory. The supporters and the team had been through some really tough times together the previous seasons, but we had finally got our reward. I cannot even begin to describe the satisfaction that gave everybody involved.

The strangest time I can remember in any dressing-room was after our defeats to New Zealand and England in the 2003 World Cup. We had given both of the favourites to win the tournament a run for their money and had finally seen all our hard work come to fruition where it mattered most – on the field. All the self-doubt and the fear that we would get ripped apart were blown away by two of the most enjoyable games of rugby I have ever played. We didn't win, but we gave the All Blacks and, in particular, the eventual world champions, England, the fright of their lives.

Sitting in a dressing-room feeling satisfied that something special has just happened, but that you have still lost, was the strangest experience. It was a new dawn for Welsh rugby and we had finally earned some self-respect in that tournament, but we had still been defeated. We had made the world sit up and take notice, were the talk of the 2003 World Cup, but were getting ready to fly home to Wales. Still, what happened that year would be the basis of the 2005 and 2008 Grand Slam successes. The foundation had been laid and a line had, at last, been drawn in the sand.

At the other end of the spectrum, Test match rugby exaggerates the feelings of failure and success. Giving your all for your country and failing is the hardest thing to bear. The physical battering you have taken for the cause suddenly overwhelms you. You feel physically broken and you are also aware there is going to be a public inquest and criticism, especially in a rugby country like Wales. Questions are asked about coaches and players, and the flak nearly always flies. People will form opinions about you when they don't know you, or what you were trying to do on the field. There is no middle ground. I have played in teams that should have won games but have been slaughtered, and in teams that were lucky to win and have been hailed as legends. The truth is somewhere in the middle. The key for every team, player and coach is not to get carried away with success or failure.

After any game, the dressing-room always looks like an accident and emergency department in a hospital in the early hours of a Saturday or Sunday morning. You see a lot of broken bodies and players with more than just casual bumps and bruises. I have known players suffer injuries that have finished their careers and I do wonder if the public really understand what professional rugby demands nowadays. There are gashes, not just cuts, to be stitched, and there are ice-packs everywhere. It is not a pretty sight. Professional rugby has been compared to a car crash, and that is pretty good comparison. Rugby is a collision sport nowadays, and if you win the collisions you win the game. While the crowd love the big hits out in the middle, there is a price to be paid after a game. Some players are totally spent; they often cannot walk and will take an age to change. Others need stitches or scans or are covered in welts and deep bruising.

I experienced the worst dressing-room for absolute carnage, where the bodies just mounted up, during the summer tour to New Zealand in 2003. We had been beaten 55–3 by the All Blacks in Hamilton, where a certain Dan Carter made his debut, and the Welsh changing room was like a scene out of a war movie. Martyn Williams required stitches to a massive gash in his cheek during the game and then had to have it re-stitched afterwards. Colin Charvis had been knocked spark out by the biggest and hardest hit I have ever seen on a rugby field, by Jerry Collins, and was sent straight to hospital. Dafydd Jones needed stitches in his private parts! That did raise a smile from a battered Welsh side and reminded us that there is always somebody worse off than you!

Daf, ironically, would have the last laugh about that. After we had lost to the All Blacks, again, at the Millennium Stadium in 2008, I jumped into the ice-bath and looked down and there was blood. On closer examination, it turned out it was my turn to have some stitches in my private parts. The joy on Daf's face had to be seen to be believed. I showed the team doctor and he said I only needed one stitch and that I didn't need a local anaesthetic. There I was, lying bollock naked on the physio table, with one of the physios putting pressure across my chest, making sure I didn't make any sudden movements. I felt the needle go in once and got ready to move, but then it went in twice and then a third time. Agony. I know adrenaline is supposed to mask any pain, but it didn't that time.

The initial joy of victory is very short-lived and it does evaporate pretty quickly. The post-mortem starts almost straight after the game. Mistakes and errors in the game are addressed. I have been in dressing-rooms where three-quarters of the side have been slapping each other on the back because they have scored a hatful of tries, but the forwards are deep in discussion, analysing why the lineout or scrum didn't come up to scratch. But then there will also always be a player who was maybe man of the match, while another knows he has had an absolute shocker and is wondering whether he will stay in the team. There are three things every player wants: to win, to play well and, of course, to get a clean bill of health. Then, if he is lucky, he will do it all over again in seven days' time.

CHAPTER 6

2005 GRAND SLAM

I failed over and over, that's why I succeed.

– Michael Jordan, six-times NBA champion

Overnight success, or the 'overnight sensation', in sport is probably the biggest myth of them all. Successful sportsmen or women and winning teams don't just appear or arrive; there has usually been a lot of blood, sweat and tears spilt on the way to achieving that goal. People are usually looking the other way when all that is going on and don't see the hard work, failure and self-doubt that are endured on the way to getting to where they want to be.

Wales's Grand Slam success in 2005 didn't just happen when we turned up for the first game against England at the Millennium Stadium. The core group of players in that team had been through more lows than probably any other national side in the history of Welsh rugby, but we had learned from our mistakes and kept together and became a mentally tough group of people. We were a squad of players that had been laughed at and mocked as the worst Wales side in history, but we stuck to our guns and got the reward.

I look back on that time as probably the most challenging, but also the most rewarding, of my career. I stop short of saying the most enjoyable because we lost ten matches in a row – every player was pushed so far out of their comfort zone and became aware he simply wasn't good enough. We were challenged like never before and, usually, found wanting. Steve Hansen got us to do one fitness test in Tenby, which was mind-blowing and took us to physical exhaustion, with no rugby benefit, just to test us mentally. Facing the fact that you are simply not good enough can be soul-destroying and humiliating. A young Wales squad dealt with that for about two years. Some players didn't complete the journey, while others just kept digging in, working hard and focusing on the job in hand. We developed a resilience and stubbornness that would stand us in good stead, and which is the hallmark of any good team. But, believe me, it wasn't easy. It didn't come overnight, and every player and coach was tested almost to breaking point.

I can remember Scott Johnson telling me years later about his first impression of the Wales squad when he turned up for his first training session at Sophia Gardens. He took one look at our physical shape and our skills levels and uttered those now immortal words: 'When does the Test team arrive, because you lot look like a pub team?'

The standard of Welsh rugby today, with the introduction of regional rugby in 2003, is so much higher than it was back at the turn of the millennium, and things will only get better. The intensity of a Scarlets versus Blues game is on another level to a Llanelli versus Cardiff club game and because of that it is so much easier to make the step up to international rugby. I can remember playing a club game against Caerphilly (no disrespect to them) one weekend and then playing a Six Nations game the next – it was no preparation for the Test arena. The Welsh rugby fans used to get very frustrated about why players who did well at club level struggled at international level and the answer is always the same: the standard of Welsh rugby wasn't good enough. It is as simple as that.

I can still remember playing for Wales against the big boys from the southern hemisphere. They would pick second-string sides against us – and we knew they had done exactly that – and they would still beat us by 40 or 50 points. Embarrassing. That certainly wouldn't happen now, and I hope it never does again. Wales, after seven years and a lot of heartache and pain, are now a team to be beaten. Wales are now a scalp other sides want, and a rugby nation to be feared again. But it didn't happen overnight.

When I first came into the national set-up, in my debut against South Africa in Pretoria in 1998, I was just happy to be there. I felt very proud to play for my country and finally pull on that famous red jersey. It was the old idea, which I think a lot of Welsh players used to have, that if you have played for Wales, you have made it. The fact that Wales suffered a humiliating record 96–13 defeat didn't even register with me – I had won my first cap and was as proud as punch. That the game had developed into tackling practice for the Welsh side didn't even come into the equation.

Looking back, my first tentative step into the choppy waters of international rugby was all about keeping my head above water. I was naive and didn't really believe I belonged. I didn't have my finger on the pulse, nor did I pay any attention to what was going on around me or what was happening outside my sphere of influence. I just wanted to soak it all up, keep my head down, learn as much as I could and stay there. That was what being successful was all about back then – don't rock the boat, don't say anything and do as you're told. Now I am very different and do take an interest, probably because I am older and more experienced and want to make sure everybody keeps raising the bar.

Phil Davies, my former Scarlets coach, always said that you can only 'control the controllables' and I have always subscribed to that view. For example, my first full international start came about because of the whole 'Grannygate' affair concerning the non-eligibility of Shane Howarth and Brett Sinkinson to play for Wales in 2000. Both had been found to have no Welsh qualification and were ruled by the International Board to be ineligible to play for Wales. That meant two key players in Graham Henry's side were now unavailable and others had to take their places in the side. It caused a huge furore at the time, but my whole focus was on how the hell I was going to fill the boots of living legend Neil Jenkins in the Wales number 10 shirt. With Jenks struggling for fitness, Howarth probably would have replaced him at fly-half because he had played there for Sale Sharks in England. With both of them sidelined, for very different reasons, it opened the door for me and a host of other players, including Rhys Williams at full-back.

I really feel for the likes of Martyn Williams and Kevin Morgan, because they went on to prove what class acts they were and could have had ten or fifteen more Welsh caps. They were the two Welsh players who'd had their path to the national team blocked by two players who weren't qualified to play for Wales. Martyn had been Brett's understudy at number 7 and has gone on to prove what a world-class rugby player he is, and Kev didn't get a look-in because Shane made the number 15 jersey his own. They probably had more reason to feel angry about it than anyone else. All I was focused on, though, was doing my best and not letting people down; the ramifications of that whole situation didn't even enter my head. I also didn't have time to soak it all up and really enjoy the occasion, even though I loved playing rugby.

I had been in the national squad since the 1999 World Cup in Wales, where I had really been a bit-part player and had come off the bench only a few times, but the whole World Cup experience was a real eye-opener. The country had been gripped with World Cup fever, and making the squad for the tournament had become a real goal for me. I had been on the summer tour as Neil Jenkins's understudy at fly-half but was strictly a squad player. Everywhere we went, everybody was talking about Wales being host of the World Cup. The hype and expectation surrounding the team went up another level and the sense of pride that we were the hosts of the tournament was very real around the whole country. The Millennium Stadium had just been finished and the buzz of excitement around the country was incredible. Wales were on a great winning streak and had beaten South Africa for the first time in the opening game at the stadium. I was one of the players who wasn't sure if I would even make the squad for the tournament, but I can still remember the sense of achievement when the letter to say I was selected dropped through the letterbox at my mother's home. I'd made it and was one of the 30 Welsh players selected for the World Cup in Wales!

Graham Henry, the former Auckland Blues coach, had been appointed in 1998 to bring back the glory days to Welsh rugby. He was the first New Zealander to coach Wales and was on a hefty salary of £250,000. With him at the helm, Wales went on a ten-match winning streak – 'the Great Redeemer' had arrived.

My first two full games for Graham were towards the end of his reign as national coach, by which time his first Wales side, which had restored real pride back into the jersey, was getting on and breaking up and had suffered with injuries. I won my first full Wales cap in 2000 against Scotland at the Millennium Stadium, playing alongside Rupert Moon, my half-back partner at Llanelli. We ground out a 26–18 win against the backdrop of the whole eligibility row. A young Shane Williams scored two tries, and I managed to get a very special memento of the game. Bill McLaren, the legendary BBC rugby commentator, was kind enough to hand me the crib sheet he'd used for that game, with all the details of the players and coaches from the game and some of his famous phrases. I had it framed and it still has pride of place on the wall at home.

The last game of the 2000 Six Nations campaign was against Ireland at Lansdowne Road. We weren't given much hope in that game, but a new-look Wales side battled to a 23–19 victory in awful conditions in Dublin. I managed to score a try, but Jenks's arrival off the bench and his ability to land a couple of pressure kicks proved the difference between the sides. We won the game and the euphoria afterwards was more a relief than anything. What I did realise, in a more reflective mood, after my first two starts for my country, was that Test match rugby was a massive jump up for me. The set-up was so much more intense. I was being challenged like never before, and knew I had some work to do, but it turned out to be much more than I thought.

Balancing pressure and opportunities is the key to professional sport at the very highest level. It's about having the courage to deal with the pressure and make the most of any opportunity you are given or work for. My first real encounter with the pressure of Test match rugby was when Graham came into the dressing-room after our defeat to Ireland at Landsdowne Road in 2002. I could see the strain on his face. I don't think people who look in from the outside really understand that the internal pressure people put themselves under is so much more intense than any external pressure.

Graham was a fantastic coach, as he proved with Wales and would prove again with New Zealand. He was professional, had great rugby knowledge and had so many innovative ideas. I was nowhere near the level he wanted, or good enough to really appreciate what a good coach he was. It is only now, years later, when something happens on the field that I think, 'Right, that was what Graham was talking about.' His technical appreciation of the game was superb; it was light years ahead of anything I had experienced before. He had a very astute rugby brain.

His attention to detail was sometimes mind-bogglingly scary. He ran moves with Wales back then that are still used now. As part of that Wales squad, it was the first time I had really been given any homework to do as a player. I wanted to get as much out of him as I could, but I did find him intimidating. He was a New Zealander, on a big salary, having arrived with a big reputation, and I didn't even know if I was ready or even up to playing Test match rugby.

It was during the Henry years, however, that I got my first real taste of what professional rugby was all about. I was a kid living the dream and just taking everything in. It was a great apprenticeship for me, but there is a part of me that regrets being so reticent around Graham and not really getting everything I could out of him. He transformed the Wales set-up and put a very good international side together, with some world-class players in their prime – some hard-nosed rugby league professionals and some great rugby athletes.

It was as part of that Wales set-up that I first really got to know Neil Jenkins and started to appreciate what a truly world-class player he was. Jenks was brilliant to me – I followed him around like a little puppy dog, hoping to find out the secrets of his success or for some of his magic to rub off on me. Jenks really broke the mould of the Welsh fly-half – luckily for me – and bore the brunt of the habitual fly-half debate in Wales. The column inches devoted to the fact he wasn't the classic 'jinking Welsh fly-half' were colossal. But, despite all of that, and his incredible mental toughness, he was approachable, generous and unselfish with me. I am sure there were times when I tested his patience, but he always had time for me and would pass on tips to help me with my game. To see his work ethic, diligence and leadership on the field was a real privilege and he left me in no doubt about what I had to do if I were ever to make the grade. He was a fantastic role model and he was Welsh. What more could I want?

Just being around the likes of Scott Quinnell, David Young and Allan Bateman, whom I had watched play rugby union in Wales and then watched play rugby league on TV, was a brilliant education for me. They knew how to switch on and switch off, how to get away from the game and not be consumed by rugby. That is a lesson I only truly appreciated much later on.

During the early part of my international career, I was tried out in a couple of positions, but I always saw myself as an outside-half. At the 2001 Six Nations, I played at full-back against England at the Millennium Stadium and, although we threw everything at the future world champions, we were on the end of a 44–15 drubbing. I knew I would never wear the number 15 jersey again after Matt Dawson left me standing like a statue in a museum with a superb step for his try. The experiment had been a disaster

– and it was a bad day at the office for yours truly. The less said about that game, the better.

The next game I would play in was against France in Paris. Jenks ran the show that day and we got another victory over Les Blues in their own backyard. I came off the bench to replace Scott Gibbs at inside centre and felt much happier there. I don't know if Graham saw me as a number 12, but I had played there before for my club and I just felt it was part of my rugby education. I was playing alongside some great players but also adjusting to the frenetic pace and claustrophobic environment of Test match rugby.

While the Lions went to Australia in the summer of 2001, Wales went to Japan on tour. I was captain when we lost the tour opener to club side Suntory in the sweltering heat of Tokyo. Even being handed ice vests at half-time to cool us down in the dressing-room didn't help. We just wilted in the heat in the second half.

We went on and beat Japan 2–0 in the Test series, but any ambitions I had when I got home about establishing myself in the Wales number 10 jersey the following season were stopped in their tracks by the arrival of Iestyn Harris. This time I was very aware of the hype, the reputed £1.5 million fee and the massive expectations on Iestyn. I remember Gareth Jenkins, my Llanelli coach, taking to me to one side and telling me I had a battle on my hands and I had to prove I was the man. I just saw Iestyn's arrival as another big challenge and one I was really looking forward to.

Jenks had come back from the Lions tour with a niggling knee injury, which would eventually end his career, and there was a vacancy at fly-half. I relished the challenge and realised there would be no pressure on me because everybody would be watching every move Iestyn made. I had nothing to lose.

The older I get, the more I realise how important competition has been to my career. It has pushed me to heights I had never dreamed of. I never had a grand plan, just dealt with the next hurdle in front of me.

I remember Iestyn's first game for Cardiff was against Llanelli at Stradey Park and he made a fantastic break. He came off the replacements bench, sidestepped second row Luke Gross, who was inside me in the defensive line, and was gone. I let Luke have it for that and made sure he knew what he'd done! Iestyn then made his first full debut for Cardiff against Glasgow at the Arms Park and had a blinder, scoring a bagful of points. The media hype went into overdrive across the rugby world. I was playing for Llanelli somewhere in Europe and can remember thinking, I have my work cut out now.

But the Welsh rugby fraternity back then was always looking for the next messiah – if it wasn't Graham, it was Iestyn. I don't know why we were like that. It meant the pressure on both of them was ridiculous. Iestyn would probably agree that his success on his first full debut for Cardiff was the worst thing that could have happened to him, because it meant people expected that from him every time he took to the pitch. It was just unrealistic. He was an instinctive rugby player, could beat a man and had amazingly quick feet, and he was deceptively strong. He was a major rugby talent and there is no doubt he fitted the bill of the romantic vision of the Welsh fly-half, but I am sure he would be the first to admit he didn't have the tactical appreciation or understanding of the role. Iestyn was a different player when he returned to league from union, though. He was a superb play-maker at number 12 and could be devastating in broken play, as he would prove at the 2003 World Cup in Australia. But before we even got to Australia, we had lost Graham as coach, and a host of senior players.

I was about to begin the darkest days, but, with hindsight, the most important part, of my career. It would be the same for so many other Welsh players in the national squad. The most popular question during the whole of that period was 'Why?' The players were asked it so many times by the coaches, then asked themselves the same question, before we would then ask the same question of the coaches. It was a brutal learning curve and one I don't think people outside will ever be able to comprehend.

Why did we lose? That was the recurring question in 2002 and 2003. The answers were painful and startlingly obvious: because we weren't fit enough, and we didn't have the physical and technical ability to perform at Test match level. What we thought was good enough plainly wasn't, and it was no surprise we came off second best all the time. It was a bitter pill to have to swallow. Everybody had given everything, but we had still lost. We had come close to winning some big games but still hadn't got the victory. We would walk off the field and sit in the dressing-room and ask ourselves, 'What do we have to do to get a win?' You start thinking you will never win a game again. 'Why are the 15 players in the opposition better than us?' They are just 15 blokes and we work as hard as them! But did we really?

Steve Hansen, another New Zealander, who had worked with the Canterbury Crusaders, had replaced Graham as head coach in 2002 and had set in motion a series of changes which would have a profound impact on the national side and Welsh rugby. Steve effectively let the likes of Scott Quinnell, Rob Howley and Dafydd James walk away from the squad. That was a massive decision because they were the best players we had. Not one of the squad agreed with Steve's decision, but he had already made a brave call to go with a young squad. With hindsight, it was a very astute move because he had a bunch of youngsters who were desperate to be a success. We were like sponges, soaking up everything he threw at us.

The first foundation stone of the success that we would enjoy much later on was laid during the Wales tour of South Africa in 2002. We lost both Tests to the Boks, though our very inexperienced side had pushed them all the way, but we had learnt we weren't fit enough. We were exposed badly in the last 20 minutes of each of those games. We knew we weren't where we needed to be physically, but at least we had played most of the rugby. Steve, Johno and Andrew Hore, our new fitness coach, were putting a plan in place and starting a process to allow us to compete against the best sides

Learning the hard way: playing football with my brother, Marc.

In my element in my Liverpool FC strip, hoping to become the next Ian Rush.

At Bro Myrddin school: the only time I've got away with long curls and a lilac shirt!

Me and Dad: he has supported me through everything.

Me and Mum, catching up after a
Wales international.

Gwen and I at a schoolmate's
wedding: there's nothing better
than catching up with friends.

Good times: I have had some good times with the Scarlets, and the challenge
now is to get us back where we belong. (© Huw Evans Picture Agency)

First try: leaving Simon Easterby, my Scarlets teammate and friend, trailing in my wake as I score my first try for my country against Ireland at Lansdowne Road in 2000. (© Huw Evans Picture Agency)

The Great Redeemer: I would only truly appreciate how good Graham Henry was as a coach much later on in my career. (© Huw Evans Picture Agency)

The Boss: Steve Hansen doing what he did best for me – telling me where I was going wrong and pointing me in the right direction. (© Huw Evans Picture Agency)

Grand Slam number one: Dwayne Peel and I celebrate Wales's first Grand Slam for 27 years in 2005 after we beat Ireland at the Millennium Stadium. We finally got our reward for the years of hard work. (© Huw Evans Picture Agency)

A second Grand Slam: doing a lap of honour to celebrate the 2008 Grand Slam with Wales after our victory over France at the Millennium Stadium. (© Huw Evans Picture Agency)

Despair: watching a penalty to clinch a win over Ireland and the Six Nations title fall just short at the Millennium Stadium. (© Huw Evans Picture Agency)

The Great Adventure: playing for Clermont against the Ospreys in the Heineken Cup. I returned to Wales a better player and a better person. (© Huw Evans Picture Agency)

The toughest day I have ever had on a rugby pitch: being a pall-bearer at Grav's funeral. Simon Easterby, Delme Thomas and I, along with Gareth Jenkins, Derek Quinnell and Dwayne Peel carried his coffin at Stradey Park.
(© Huw Evans Picture Agency)

Rivals, but brothers in arms for the Lions: Ronan O'Gara and I discuss tactics after a training session with the Lions on the 2009 South Africa tour. We have had some great battles over the years, but we have a mutual respect for each other. (© Inpho Sports Photography)

Now or never: Warren Gatland, the Wales coach and assistant coach with the Lions, delivers the half-time team talk in the dressing-room in Jo'burg before we salvage pride, if not the Test series, against the Springboks.
(© Inpho Sports Photography)

Pain and despair: lost in thought after losing the first Test in Durban. The names over my shoulder of the great Lions number 10s are a reminder of what a privilege it is to wear that jersey. (© Inpho Sports Photography)

The legacy: I have just landed the penalty to level the scores, with minutes to go, in the second Test in Pretoria against the Boks, with my great friend Neil Jenkins supporting me throughout. Morne Steyn's penalty would win the Test, and the Test series, for South Africa minutes later.
(© Inpho Sports Photography)

The Icemen: Even Lions have to use the dreaded ice bath. Brian O'Driscoll, Jamie Roberts and me after a training session with the Lions in South Africa in 2009. (© Inpho Sports Photography) in the world. They had taken a look at us and knew we were never going to be a physical team, so wouldn't have the ability to bully or steamroller teams. It amazed me that people didn't pick up on the thought, detail and courage they showed to come up with a style of play to fit the players they had. Coaches usually do it the other way around: they come up with a style of play and fit players into the style they want to play.

Steve used to bang the drum about performance rather than results, and he took some flak for that publicly, but he was right. What he was saying was that we weren't good enough physically, technically or tactically to expect to win Test matches against the big boys of world rugby, but if a side that isn't good enough performs to the best of its ability, you cannot ask for more. We simply weren't good enough back then. None of the players liked it, but his analysis was right. We went on a ten-match losing streak and it was an embarrassment. We were, effectively, not good enough at our jobs. Nobody likes that in any walk of life, let alone when you are representing your national team in its national sport. You just feel you are letting everybody down.

Steve sheltered us from a lot of what was happening outside the set-up, but everybody knew the flak was flying his way. The only answer for the players was to become engrossed in the process. Ignorance is bliss, as they say. So, that's what we did. The national set-up had become a no-holds-barred environment and a challenging place to be, where everybody was expected to take responsibility for what happened on and off the pitch. While the rest of Welsh rugby was talking about addressing the needs of professional sport, the national side was doing exactly that. The debate about regional rugby was at its height, there had been threatened strike action by players and Wales had 'won' the wooden spoon in the 2003 Six Nations. Not a great time to be a rugby player in Wales. But behind closed doors, despite the run of dismal defeats, things had started to change. We had started to develop the tightness and mental toughness needed at the highest level.

Steve, in particular, had no qualms about telling you things you didn't want to hear, and that became part of the squad culture.

Personally, it was an exciting, exhilarating and exhausting time for me. I was testing myself against some of the best and very different number 10s in the business. Carlos Spencer, Jonny Wilkinson, Felipe Contepomi, Stephen Larkham, Ronan O'Gara and Gregor Townsend all tested me and exposed weaknesses in my game. The video analysis afterwards was always pretty painful. Why was I doing that? Why hadn't I moved? Why did I kick then? But it was all part of my rugby education. I wanted to test myself against the best and I had to learn the number 10 position wasn't a personal battle, like it is for a prop or a hooker or a winger. It didn't matter if I played really well and the team lost. I had to get the best out of every situation on the field and make decisions that were good for my teammates and the team. It was a real kick up the arse for me.

The 2003 season would prove to be a watershed for the squad and Welsh rugby in general. This was demonstrated before the 2003 summer tour to Australia and New Zealand, when the squad refused to get on the plane because of another pay cut for the tour. I still smile when I remember Scott Quinnell, who was chairman of the Welsh Rugby Players' Association, coming to see the whole squad in a service station after we had refused to get on the team bus and asking how many of us wanted to go on the tour. Everybody put their hand up and we soon got on the bus. We all had to pay our own hotel bill at Heathrow because we had missed the flight. But something had happened during the build-up to the World Cup: the whole squad had matured. Steve, Johno and Horey had had us for 32 of the 52 weeks building up to the tournament and their message was starting to get through. We got hammered by the All Blacks in Hamilton on that tour but did hold our own against the Wallabies, despite being beaten in the end.

Our next trip Down Under was for my second World Cup and it was one of the most enjoyable experiences of my career. The coaches had organised for the likes of Glenn McGrath, the legendary Aussie cricketer, along with three rugby league legends – Wally Lewis, Andrew 'Joey' Johns and Mal Meninga – and General Peter Cosgrove to speak to us. Why any of them would come to speak to us, or even take the time to talk to us, was beyond most of us, but it was inspirational stuff. Players who were voted man of the match would get a cricket bat signed by Steve Waugh, the Australian cricket captain, or a signed didgeridoo.

We stayed in self-catering apartments in Canberra, where we were based, and nobody really took any notice of us. We were pretty much left to our own devices. I don't think many Aussies knew the Wales rugby team were in their city. I shared with Colin Charvis, the Wales captain, who does a great cooked breakfast, though you don't really want to be caught cooking it when your fitness coach and nutritionist walk in. Brent Cockbain, our Aussie-born Welsh second row, was the chef of the squad, though. He baked cakes and made these unbelievable homemade chutneys for everybody. We all wanted to be invited to Cobber's place for food while we were in the Australian capital!

During the Pool stages, we were still working hard on our fitness and managed to get a few unsatisfactory wins over Tonga, Canada and Italy, which meant we would play England in the quarter-finals in Brisbane. Before that, it was New Zealand in Sydney. We had already qualified for the knockout stages and the pressure, to a certain extent, was off. We had set a goal of a quarter-final place and had achieved that, but what happened next surprised everybody.

We hadn't played particularly well in our earlier Pool games, though we had won them all. People underestimate what winning can do for a side's confidence. Against the All Blacks and England, somehow, everything we had trained for and worked so hard to perfect, just came to fruition on the pitch. Everybody had written us off before the All Blacks game, expecting them to turn up and win by a cricket score, but everything just fell into place for us. Shane Williams had one of those games you dream about and we just played attacking rugby against the best attacking rugby side in the world. Suddenly, Wales were the talk of the tournament. We had given the favourites a real game and the style of rugby we had played had caught everybody's imagination.

It was England next up in Brisbane, and suddenly people who had ignored us for most of the tournament started to take an interest in Wales. We were so relaxed before the England game, a few of us went off surfing for the day, ignoring Horey's directive about staying out of the sun and conserving energy for the big game. We came back absolutely knackered and sunburnt, but had had a great day away from all the hype in the build-up to the game. It's a classic example of how relaxed we felt.

Once again, we played all the rugby and I finished off a try after some great running lines and passing by Shane, Gareth Cooper and Gareth Thomas. I just had to flop over the line after running half the length of the field in support, but we had stunned everybody. We would eventually lose 28–17, but we had played all the rugby. I would get an award for scoring the try of the 2003 World Cup in Australia. England, in the second half, reverted to type and played a much more conservative style than us and just wore us down physically. England would win the 2003 World Cup against Australia, but another foundation stone had been laid in the Welsh revival.

I am very proud of what we achieved in that tournament, but we still hadn't won a big game against one of the big boys of Test match rugby. We were a very young team and, although we had started to win games we should have been winning, we were also losing games we had a chance of winning. Success breeds success and Wales were a team trying to get somewhere we hadn't been before. We weren't a great team and we knew that, and we were now in uncharted territory. Very few of us knew what it felt like to win the big games. Call it inexperience, lack of self-belief or lack of confidence; we just didn't know how to win when the pressure was really on. We would bridge that gap, but it would take a while yet.

The 2004 Six Nations came and went and was memorable because Steve Hansen, for so long pilloried by everybody, got a great send-off and the one he deserved. Everybody made it pretty clear they wanted him to stay in Wales, but the lure of coaching the All Blacks was too strong. It was totally understandable, and the important thing was that Johno and Horey had agreed to stay with us. Wales hadn't really done succession planning or transition before because most coaches had quit or been sacked. I was delighted that Johno and Horey were still on board, because too many changes can hurt a side; you don't need to go looking for a new group of leaders all the time. It's much better to manage the situation. Welsh rugby had done boom and bust before.

But the appointment of Mike Ruddock ahead of my Scarlets coach, Gareth Jenkins, took everybody by surprise, including me. I had just assumed Gareth was going to get the job. The Scarlets were the most successful and probably the strongest side in Wales. It was certainly the strongest Scarlets side I had played for. I was looking forward to working with Gareth, so was shocked when Mike was finally unveiled as Wales coach.

There has been a lot of talk about the whys and wherefores of the whole situation. I understand why the Welsh Rugby Union wanted to keep Johno and Horey. They had been absolutely vital to the squad. I still believe Gareth and Johno, in particular, would have made a formidable coaching team. For me, they were almost a perfect mix. But it's understandable that Gareth wanted his own coaching team around him. Every coach wants that. Although Gareth and Johno are such big characters and intuitively understand the nuances of the game, I still believe it would have been an irresistible combination. They would have had so many ideas and been so innovative; nobody will ever persuade me it wouldn't have been a fantastic partnership! They are both rugby fanatics and infectious rugby people. Like everybody in West Wales, I really felt for Gareth when he didn't get the job. Professional sport is so unpredictable, nothing surprises me any more.

The autumn Test series in 2004 was another of those foundation stones. We managed to push New Zealand and South Africa all the way and just fell short of getting a big scalp. Throughout those games, I could feel that the whole side had gone up a level: the fear factor of playing the Blacks and the Boks had gone. Our fitness was such that we finished really strongly against both of them. We weren't getting bullied or thrown around like rag dolls any more. My abiding memory of that autumn campaign is watching Colin Charvis at close hand taking lumps out of Richie McCaw, the All Blacks openside. Charv was immense in that game. We didn't know it, but something special was around the corner.

People often ask me, 'Did you know you were going to win a Grand Slam in 2005, was there a feeling that something special was going to happen during that Six Nations campaign?' The honest answer is no. As a player, you are just so caught up in the process of trying to improve that sometimes you forget how far you have travelled. You get consumed by the merry-go-round and forget to take in the view. The victory against England certainly got the ball rolling and, of course, Gavin Henson announced himself on the world stage and landed a mammoth penalty. I didn't play particularly well in that game and, despite kicking well for Clermont, didn't have a great game with the boot.

I can remember there was a big debate about whether Gav should be the frontline kicker before the game against Italy in Rome. Johno, in typical fashion, then told me I was kicking against the Italians. As he walked away, with a mischievous smile, he warned me not to miss. I got my first kick over, but it was our attacking play that was sublime during that game. We were a side playing with utter confidence in ourselves, each other and the system we were playing. But the turning point – when we started thinking about the possibility of a Grand Slam – was the victory over France in Paris. The French boys gave us a physical battering in the first half and threw the kitchen sink at us. We wouldn't have been able to cope with such a physical examination before: we would have withdrawn into our shells, battened down the hatches and gone into damage-limitation mode. If the Italy game had been about fantasy rugby, the game against France was the other side of the coin. This was all about character, having the courage of our convictions and refusing to take a step back. We tackled everything that moved but played high-tempo rugby, and our commitment to that approach summed up the psyche of the team. There were some great personal battles, and the one between Shane and Aurelien Rougerie, my teammate at Clermont, typified the great contrasts of the game of rugby. It was a clash of styles – Rougerie's power and pace against Shane's quick feet – and is why the game fascinates so many people. I can remember Rougerie taking a ball off the first scrum and running straight at me.

At half-time we were hanging on, but there was no panic or great team talk in the dressing-room. We dealt with the facts. We knew they were uncomfortable when we had the ball in our hands and that we just needed more of the ball to cause them real problems. What we didn't do was crumble, like we had done so many times before. Martyn Williams scored a couple of tries and we survived a major onslaught towards the end of the game, but we had shown we had finally learnt the hard lessons of the previous seasons. I was man of the match and we had taken another big scalp.

We were three wins out of three games and now talk of a Grand Slam was on everybody's lips. Scotland has been a bad hunting ground for us, but everything we did came off and we ran out comfortable winners. I don't think we could have put a foot wrong if we had tried. Beating Ireland at the Millennium Stadium and winning the first Grand Slam for Wales since 1978 was just an overwhelming feeling. None of us felt we could lose that game. We had found a rhythm and were playing out of our skins. There had been all sorts of people – players, coaches and staff – who had played their part in that success and some of them weren't even with us any more.

Welsh rugby, for so long written-off, had re-emerged and was being taken seriously again. Just as importantly, we were playing a brand of rugby in the best traditions of the Welsh game. We had a pack that could compete and a back line that wanted to attack, but all of us could pass and offload in the tackle. For those of us who had been through the dark days, it was a deeply satisfying moment.

What always made me smile was all the talk that Wales had rediscovered 'the Welsh way' of playing and had shown the power game wasn't the only way to win games. The fact that three of the key people in forging that style were from the southern hemisphere was lost on most people. They had analysed our strengths and weaknesses and come up with a style of play that had evolved over three years to suit the players they had. It sounds simple, but it took real guts and vision to do that. We couldn't play a power game. Players had to be fit, skilful, good technically and tactically astute to deliver the style of rugby that won the Grand Slam.

What made it so special for me was that we were probably playing fantasy rugby and we were winning by passing the ball. We were a side full of confidence and executed moves that were ridiculously complex, but we just gave it a go and it came off. We were playing high-risk rugby and knew that we were putting ourselves under pressure, knew a mistake in front of 70,000 people would make us all look stupid, but confidence was sky high and we just wanted to play and push ourselves to even greater heights. We knew what we had to do and we knew how to do it.

I believe the 2005 Grand Slam left a very real legacy to Welsh rugby. So many doubted what Steve and Horey, in particular, had pinpointed as the weaknesses of Welsh rugby, but after that success the genie was out of the bottle. I know I certainly didn't really appreciate the detail that went into creating a strong and robust rugby environment, culture or even national side. It opened my eyes and those of many others in Welsh rugby. Now, we understand how important good facilities are and how important support staff are for a squad. All these things may be boring for those on the outside, but they are critical to any success we enjoy now or in the future. The Scarlets, the Ospreys and the Blues have fantastic set-ups, and it's probably only the Dragons who are playing catch-up, but we have a system now which rivals any other country in the rugby world.

Once upon a time, the best teams in Wales were miles off their counterparts around the world. Now, the Welsh regions could definitely hold their own against a Super 14 team. The gap has closed.

CHAPTER 7

PLAYER POWER

It's a hard life as a professional cricketer. It's not as easy as everyone makes out. To survive, you need a tough hide.

– Steve Waugh, former Australian cricket captain
and the most-capped Test player in history

February 2006 will always be remembered as the year when a new phrase entered the vocabulary of Welsh rugby: 'player power'. And it was blamed for Mike Ruddock's departure as Wales coach. I always found it ironic that before we won the Grand Slam in 2005 our level of performance was due to the lack of leaders in the Welsh team, but then a so-called 'cabal of players' had ganged up on a Grand Slam coach and forced him out of his job.

I was out of the way in France when the whole situation blew up and the first I knew of Mike's resignation was through a host of texts on my phone, telling me he was no longer Wales coach. I was as shocked as everybody else at his decision. This whole episode was a steep learning curve for everybody in the Wales squad.

Welsh rugby thrives on rumour, speculation, drama and sometimes utter nonsense. I have heard all sorts of theories and stories about Mike's departure and most of them are unbelievable. One of them is that the players were jealous of his success. Why?

Financially, we had all done well out of the Grand Slam, were all feted as national heroes and had the kudos of being Grand Slam winners on our CVs. We had the satisfaction of a job well done and there was certainly no jealousy towards Mike.

He was the coach at the helm and nobody could, or should, take that away from him. The record books will show that Mike was the Wales coach who won the Grand Slam in 2005. Nobody can argue with that. The facts don't lie.

Much has been made of a meeting that Gareth Thomas, Martyn Williams, Brent Cockbain and I had with Steve Lewis, the Welsh Rugby Union's chief executive, at the time. It was during this get-together that we were supposed to have undermined our coach. The meeting was called to address an insurance issue the players had about an injury to scrum-half Gareth Cooper, and we also made it very clear to Steve that the players wanted to make sure everything was done to keep Scott Johnson, who was the Wales skills coach, with the national set-up.

Johno had some personal family issues he had to deal with back home in Sydney in Australia and had made it clear it was becoming hard for him to stay in Wales. We had already lost Andrew Hore, our fitness coach, in the autumn of 2005 after our Grand Slam success, as he had returned to work for the New Zealand Rugby Union. We had beaten Australia for the first time in donkey's years that November and were ready to take the next step as a squad. Both Johno and Horey had been key to our success and I am sure Mike would be the first to admit that. Losing them both in a short space of time, especially then, when the team needed continuity and stability, was going to leave a big hole in the national set-up.

I am sure Steve, like any boss of any business, wanted to know what was going on on the shop floor, but the idea it was the moment when a plot was hatched to get rid of Mike is ludicrous. We made our feelings known about how important Johno was, but I don't think our meeting was the reason Mike left. There was talk of issues with his new contract with the WRU being a problem, but I honestly know nothing about that. I still feel we were duty-bound to make the voice of the players heard, but we all learned a valuable lesson during that period. One of the results was that the whole squad became much tighter, and there is a real unity there now.

I would like to think that Mike would be the first to admit that he inherited a squad that was on an upward curve, one that had grown up together between 2002 and 2005. There is no doubt that the 2006 Six Nations was a very different campaign from the 2005 Grand Slam. We had been decimated by injuries, with a host of players missing due to operations. The previous summer there had been a Lions tour to New Zealand and there is always fallout after a gruelling trip like that. Players who had been key parts of our success were missing and new players such as Mike Phillips, Hal Luscombe and Matthew Watkins were drafted into the set-up. They were being asked to make a big step up and it always takes time for players to find their feet at Test match level. I just remember it being a really tough time and a very frustrating period for everybody in the squad, including Mike and Johno. We all wanted to build on the success we had enjoyed and go up a level. I certainly felt that way because we all wanted to build on the success we'd had the previous season. It just didn't happen.

I make no bones about the fact that I was very close to Johno and wanted him to stay in Wales, but he had a very difficult family situation to deal with back home in Australia at the time. I know there was a lot of speculation about the fact that Johno and Mike's relationship wasn't as strong as it had been at the beginning, but I cannot comment on something I don't know about. Did I see their relationship deteriorate towards the end? Well, if they had any disagreements, they certainly kept it away from us, but if there were cracks in their relationship, the victory over Australia at the Millennium Stadium in the autumn of 2005 probably papered over them.

Personally, I did feel we weren't progressing as we should have been and that we had slipped into a comfort zone, something that was levelled at the team in the media at the time. With hindsight, perhaps I was unrealistic, thinking we could keep improving at the rate of knots we had done in the previous seasons. All I know is that all the players were desperate to kick on and build on the success we'd enjoyed; we were all very conscious that we were on the brink of something special. We didn't want to wallow in that success or bask in the glory of a Grand Slam. We all knew Welsh rugby's reputation for boom-and-bust and were desperate to build sustained and consistent success for the national side. Ironically, the opposite happened.

I was lucky to be playing in France and away from everything that was happening in Wales. All I knew was that there had been great hype in Wales about our success, and I will be the first to admit I got frustrated with our lack of progress afterwards because our performances just levelled off. We seemed to be happy with our lot. I wanted to keep improving and go to the next level.

Perhaps I was naive and didn't appreciate that we weren't as good as I thought we were. I know some people claim Mike was the reason we won the Grand Slam, and I have no real argument with that. The facts are the facts. Mike was a Grand Slam coach. People often speculate whether Wales would have won the Grand Slam if Steve Hansen had still been in charge in 2005 and had not returned to New Zealand to join Graham Henry's back-room team with the All Blacks. Who knows? It's all speculation and it's irrelevant, because he wasn't. Mike was.

Steve and Johno are very different characters; there is no doubt about that. Steve could be a pain in the arse and was a stickler for everything, always challenging the players and pushing us. He was a former policeman and was pretty intense, but was almost like a human shield for the squad when we were losing. He didn't allow the external pressure to even penetrate the squad. He built a wall around us and protected all of the players from any the criticism that was being thrown at us.

Johno was always looking for new ideas and new ways of doing things from different sports, and he is an Aussie, so he never had any trouble calling a spade a spade. He certainly wasn't trying to be the players' friend, as he has often been described, and wouldn't spare your feelings if you had done something wrong. He always explained selection decisions though, and told you what you had to improve on. He was a very good technical coach and broke down the game very well, and he was great in a one-on-one situation. He saw little things in your game and would adapt them, improve them or even get rid of them. Steve and Johno are often described as a classic 'good cop, bad cop' double act, but it was never as black and white as that.

I am pretty sure they had some lively discussions and vigorous debates when they worked together with Wales. Neither of them was a shrinking violet and they always challenged each other and pushed each other. They also certainly didn't agree on everything and had no qualms saying when the other needed to pull his finger out. They were very similar but also very different, if that makes sense. They would work all the hours they could to make sure we were the best prepared we could be. Their incredible work ethic rubbed off on the whole squad. If they were doing it, we had to. They had both made their homes in Wales and had arrived at a time when Welsh rugby was really struggling to come to terms with the professional era and what was needed to be a success in the modern game. They learnt everything about Welsh rugby they could. They went to see regional games, Welsh players playing outside the country and age-group rugby within Wales. The pair of them, along with Horey, built up an incredible knowledge of current players and young players to be monitored.

There were a few episodes during that whole period which had a profound impact on me, and I know they had the same effect on the rest of the squad. The way Johno was pilloried in public really upset me and left a bad taste in my mouth. Here was a guy who had done so much for Welsh rugby and all of a sudden he was public enemy number one. The other was Alfie's grilling on TV about the whole situation. I was in France at the time, but his decision to front up and defend his players was classic Alfie. As captain, he felt it was his duty to protect his team and his players, and I cannot fault him for that. He loved being Wales captain and loved his team. He certainly took the bullets for all of us on that day. He did leave himself exposed by agreeing to appear and, afterwards, all the players felt he had been ambushed. The disappointing thing about watching all of that unfold was that you felt the opinions of the people involved had already been formed and nothing Alfie could have said would have changed their views. Hindsight is a wonderful thing, but I firmly believe now that two players should have done that show.

I remember at the time everybody seemed qualified to comment on 'a players' revolt' in the Wales squad. The whole team, who had been feted as national heroes less than 12 months before, were now painted as villains. Everybody seemed intent on dividing the squad and there was no middle ground at all. Players were getting grilled and accused of all sorts of things during that time and being expected to defend themselves, when everybody had decided we were already guilty and responsible for what had happened. People tried to pick us off, but when you are part of a team, you are always part of a team.

I found that whole time, and its aftermath, profoundly upsetting. Morale in the camp fluctuated so much during that period, and it took all of us a long time to get over what happened. It brought all of the players closer together. It was a massive learning curve for all of us. We all developed pretty thick skins after and I think the new mental toughness can be seen in the current Wales squad.

The whole 'Ruddockgate' saga did underline how rugby had changed since the introduction of professionalism. The level of scrutiny players and coaches are under by the media is now huge. The story was on the front and back pages and was the lead item on news programmes; it underlined just how big the game had become. Players today are well paid to do their jobs and the hype around the game is on another planet. They and the coaches are under the spotlight like never before, and every decision is analysed and debated over and over. The reaction to victory and defeat has become more emotional than I can ever remember, but that is because the profile of the game has rocketed out of sight. I have learnt to deal with that and am now pretty good at switching off after a win or a loss, but, with the high profile, there are now loads of pitfalls for young players trying to make their way in the game. I would like to think I have managed to avoid most of them . . . just.

I am a sports fanatic and always watch sport on TV. I could watch four or five rugby games over a weekend, if I wanted to. But I don't think having so many live games on TV has helped the sport. When people stay at home to watch rugby, it means players sometimes play in half-empty stadiums. That cannot be good for anybody, though I understand that TV deals are now the backbone of most professional sports, and rugby is no different.

Just like everybody, I love to hear what is supposed to be going on or who is moving to this club, but I do take a lot of it with a pinch of salt. My experience has always been that sometimes the media is spot on and sometimes it's miles off. I respect the role of the media in the promotion of the game, and that I have a duty, as a professional player and a Welsh international, to promote the game, but I am much more aware of the consequences of victory and defeat and the impact it can have on every side I play for. People's livelihoods are now at stake.

The days of turning up for a pre-season team photo and just playing a game every weekend are long gone. Now there are pre-match press conferences and interviews to be done and post-match press conferences and TV and radio interviews. The exposure and profile of rugby players, especially in Wales, has exploded. I worry when I see younger players get caught up in all the media hype and start to live their life in the glare of publicity. I wouldn't say I have deliberately shunned the spotlight, but I have always appreciated there is a life away from rugby. Players are put up on a pedestal and can get anything and everything they want if they play well in Wales, but fame, or whatever, has never really interested me. Nobody dies if I don't get selected in a team, or if my team loses, or if I play badly.

I don't have a problem with players enjoying their moment in the sun, but it does raise a wry smile when they start complaining about the bad press they have had or criticisms they receive when they have made a mistake on the pitch or played badly. I have never heard a player complain when he has read a good article or heard nice things said about him on TV or radio. I have always believed if you liked it when it was good, you have to put up with it when it's bad. I respect other people's opinions when they are based on facts, but have little time when people just seem to want to court controversy. Some players like to live their life in the spotlight and others have very little choice, but I have always wanted my personal life to be my personal life. The bottom line for me will always be the rugby, and how I perform on the pitch. I still believe that is the key to everything.

I want the respect of my peers and my opponents, above all else. If a player is enjoying all the attention, and it's not hurting his rugby or detrimental to the team, let him enjoy it. Some players, though, are built up by the media just to be knocked down and I don't understand that. And sometimes the media image of a player doesn't come close to where he actually is as a player.

Professional players have to look after themselves because rugby is now their job, of course. It's a short career and I know that my earning power will be cut drastically when I retire from the game. That's why players have a rugby agent to look after their contract with their club, region or province, and even a commercial agent to look after any other deals they have outside rugby. I have a great deal with my boot supplier Adidas, and I'm very happy with that. When I started, I might have got a free pair of boots, but that was all. I don't think there is a wrong or right way to deal with the profile available to rugby players; I just know it has no appeal to me and it won't make me happier. I don't want my rugby, or my life, to be driven by too many outside influences.

My respect for rugby supporters and the money they spend to follow and support any team will always be of the utmost. I have seen it with the Scarlets, Clermont, Wales and the Lions. Seeing them make the effort to follow their team does make it hit home the responsibility you have, as a player, to perform. I find it humbling. Most supporters are as good as gold, but I can remember one bad experience, and that was in Wales. We had lost to Ireland in Dublin and one fan came over to abuse us as we were picking up our bags after the disappointing defeat, but that was a rare instance. When you have walked through the patrons' bar at Stradey Park after a game, it prepares you for most things. All the players used to have to walk through the supporters to get something to eat after a game, and by the time you had picked up your food you knew how you'd played! It was the same when I started playing for Carmarthen. The old veterans of the club would have no qualms about telling you if you'd played like a clown!

The higher up the ladder you climb in rugby, the more exposed you are. I am more aware of people taking pictures on their mobile phones than I ever was before, or trying to take advantage of you, but it all comes with the territory.

Test match rugby is exactly that: it is a test of everything about you as a rugby player and a person. It's a test of skill, ability, character and mental strength. It's a test of how you handle what happens on the field, and even what happens off it. It's like a drug. And the positive experiences always outweigh the negative ones for me.

I still play the game because I love it. If I didn't, I wouldn't still be playing. But I am from a different era. I have been very lucky, as I didn't expect to make a career out of rugby. Now teenagers come into the game wanting to make a living out of the game. I never had that kind of pressure when I started out. I just jumped the next hurdle in front of me and have tried to make the most of all the opportunities that have come my way.

I still enjoy the process of playing rugby, and working out why something works and why it doesn't. All that matters is what I do during the 80 minutes on the pitch. How I am perceived or marketed is really irrelevant to me. I just want to be respected for what I do as a rugby player on the pitch.

CHAPTER 8

THE WORKING WEEK

You aren't born a professional. You have to turn yourself into one. You have to do the right things. You have to eat right, you have to sleep right.

– Lance Armstrong, seven-times Tour de France winner

I am one of a dying breed of rugby player, who has seen the best of the amateur days and had the best professional rugby can offer. I have, quite literally, had the best of both worlds. I have played a game on a Saturday afternoon and then gone out and got hammered with my teammates, win or lose. Likewise, I have stood in an ice-bath, loaded up on supplements provided by the team's nutritionist after a game, and woken up early the following morning after a game to do a pool recovery session. I have had a brown envelope full of cash handed to me after a game and now have an accountant and a solicitor to look after my rugby contracts and personal sponsors. As an amateur, pre-1996, I ate and drank what I wanted, when I wanted, and had no idea what the life of a professional sportsman, let alone rugby player, was all about. I can go months now without touching a drop of alcohol, but there was a time when I used to have five or six pints straight after a game on a Friday night and then meet up on a Saturday afternoon and drink all the way through until the early hours. Some of the drinking sessions with Simon and Guy Easterby and Matt Cardey at the Scarlets are legendary. I would have Sunday to recover and then go back to work on a Monday. I thought that was acceptable behaviour for a rugby player at the time. I didn't know, let alone appreciate, what I was doing to my body's ability to recover from playing a game of rugby. Now, I lead the life of a professional rugby player and look after my body, watch what I eat and don't touch alcohol for three days before I play. I still like a drink, like everybody else, but there is a time and a place in the season when it's acceptable.

When I got my first 'professional' contract with Llanelli as a teenager, I was still playing social rugby and had no idea what being a real professional meant. I can remember turning up for my first pre-season fitness session and failing to complete it three times because I was so unfit. I had been on a two-week holiday to Magaluf in Spain with the boys and I turned up with ginger hair after trying to dye it blond. Looking like a clown with ginger hair probably didn't help either. I was a boy in a man's world. I was just paid to play rugby and that's what I did. I didn't really have any understanding or comprehension about the sacrifices I had to make to be successful. For me, and so many other players in Wales at the time, being paid to play meant you were successful already. I shudder when I look back at how naive I was at the start of my career, but I wouldn't change my experience at all. I was, like so many Welsh players in the professional era, a guinea pig, as Wales tried to understand and come to grips with what professionalism meant. I have seen so many fads, short cuts and magic formulas designed to make us better players, which never worked and were never going to work.

There can be so much nonsense talked about in rugby and in particular the Welsh rugby fraternity loved looking for the magic formula or the quick-fix when the answer was always about working hard. If it wasn't one player or one coach who was going to lead us to the Promised Land, it was sweet potatoes or the weather! Finally, we have got over that, but it took nearly a decade for us to get to grips with the professional game and it was only the influx of overseas rugby thinking which educated us about the real rugby issues, that saw us develop and become a proper rugby nation again.

Now players have a choice if they want to be a professional rugby player in Wales, and that means making sacrifices and living the life of a professional athlete. That's the deal and it's the way it should be. If you want to be a social rugby player, you can still do that, but being professional means being very strict, disciplined and hard on yourself. The old 'work hard, play hard' mentality just doesn't apply any more.

The change in the rugby culture in Wales over the last decade has been dramatic. It's now a no-excuses environment, and you have to be dedicated to your career if you want to be successful – no stone is left unturned. If you don't have that dedication, somebody else will come along who has and he will take your place. Rugby is now a job and a livelihood.

Dieticians, nutritionists and chefs are an integral part of the back-up team for any squad. Players are told what to eat and when to replenish to make sure their body is always being looked after. The attention to detail now is simply astounding, but, for me, it has become a habit and part of my lifestyle. There are also the dreaded ice-baths, which I detest, but I know are good for me, after training and games to aid physical recovery. Players wear compression garments these days while travelling after a game, and rest and recovery have become key parts of the life of a professional. Players may be paid to train and play, but they are also paid to rest in the right way and look after their bodies – that means rounds of golf, running around all day, drinking too much alcohol and eating junk food are not an option any more. Otherwise you are wasting all the good work you have done and there will be an impact on your body when you train and play. It is that simple.

The life of a professional rugby player is now all about being self-disciplined and regimented; absolutely nothing is left to chance. Even training sessions have changed out of sight compared with when I first started in the game. Since we were being paid, people thought we should train nine-to-five, five days a week, before playing on a Saturday. The days of rugby training sessions lasting for hours, which was what happened when the game first went pro, and hanging around on the pitch for ages not really doing anything, are long gone. Training sessions today are short and sharp and may only last an hour, but are now done at match intensity.

Analysis is also a much bigger and more important part of the game than it has ever been. Teams, players, phases of play, and attacking and defensive strategies are all analysed in minute detail. Games have never been broken down or chewed over in the way they are now. Every player has a laptop and can analyse the game and his personal performance almost immediately after the final whistle. The detail is mind-boggling, when I compare it with the early days of video recorders and watching a tape of a game on a TV with the whole squad.

There is a danger of paralysis by analysis, but generally most coaches and players know what they are looking for and what key areas they are focusing on in a game. Now you get a printout of the team stats and your own personal stats. You get told how many tackles you made, even how many of them were positive, or game-changing; you know how many tackles you made with your right or left shoulder, how many times you passed off your left or right hand. Then there are the kicks: how many you made, whether it was grubbers, restarts, goal-kicking, drop kicks or chip kicks. The whole game will be broken down in such a scientific way as to give you the real facts of your performance.

The success of a team or a player will always depend on the talent and intelligence of the other players in the team and of the team as a whole, but everybody is looking for the little 1 per cents to give them the edge in a game. Sides are now so professional that those 1 per cents are what everybody is searching for and they can make the difference between winning and losing, or coaches staying in a job or being sacked.

When I started out, so much of rugby training was team-orientated. We would have a team rugby session or a team fitness session. Now the game is tailored more towards the individual needs of a position and a player and everyone has their own personal training programme. Rugby has always been a game for all shapes, sizes and ages, and that hasn't really changed in the professional game. Everything has been broken down in a very scientific way for each position and each body type.

The three people who, I believe, had the biggest impact on Welsh rugby are Steve Hansen, Scott Johnson and Andrew Hore. They transformed the working week of every rugby player in Wales. Personally, I don't think Steve has had, or will ever get, the credit he deserves for turning Welsh rugby around. Professional rugby in Wales didn't start in 1995 when the game went professional, but when Steve arrived in 2002. We were so off the mark when it came to the global game.

On a personal level, Steve kept pushing and challenging me, and he did that with every other player, too. He was a very shrewd bloke and mentally a tough character, who brought so many good habits from the Canterbury Crusaders in New Zealand to the Wales set-up. He challenged the Welsh players like no other coach had at the time. He was brutally honest and educated us about what the life of a professional athlete was all about. He had incredibly high standards and really did, quite literally, break the mould of a Welsh rugby player and rebuild it.

Nobody pissed me off more than Steve while he was Wales coach. With hindsight, everything he said about being professional and about my game was spot on. When I look back, Steve was so right about the problems with Welsh players and Welsh rugby. Nobody kicked me up the arse more than he did. I didn't like hearing what he had to say at the time, but he always told the truth and if you didn't like it, it was your problem. None of us likes hearing the truth, especially when it's very negative, but that doesn't mean it isn't the truth. We like to put our heads in the sand and ignore the negative stuff, but Steve forced all the players to take a long, hard look at themselves. I had to learn the hard way from him, but his time in charge forced the steepest learning curve of my career.

Everybody in Welsh rugby thought what we were doing was good enough, but it clearly wasn't. It's hard to even understand how arrogant everybody – players, coaches, administrators, supporters – was in thinking we were anywhere near where we needed to be. Our skills might have been good enough to succeed in Wales and get a professional contract, but they would never have got any Welsh player a contract anywhere else in the world.

Before Steve, Johno and Horey arrived in Wales, I had experienced so many hare-brained schemes designed to put us back on the rugby map. Welsh rugby had always been obsessed with copying something totally irrelevant from Australia, New Zealand, South Africa or England which was meant to transform the national side. It was always the same – they are doing this, so we have to do it. It was never about fitness or skill, rather to do with them eating more red meat in South Africa or Australia having better weather and a great climate. It was all rubbish and not quantifiable. It seemed like pure laziness. In my view, most of it was an excuse for not working hard enough.

Steve and Johno were, in particular, a great double act while they were with Wales, but it was Horey who was the real taskmaster and he could be brutal when it came to fitness. He transformed rugby fitness in Wales. I still cringe when I remember the first fitness session he took with the Wales squad and the look on his face at the end of it. He couldn't believe what he was seeing. He was in a state of shock at the fitness of the players he had to work with.

Horey had come from the Canterbury Crusaders in New Zealand, where the side was made up of 90 per cent of the All Blacks. He was used to working with the best of the best. What he got when he arrived in Wales was a group of players doing weights like bodybuilders. That was just no good for a rugby player. His approach to fitness was a real eye-opener for all of us. I can remember when he first handed out a monthly fitness schedule and diary to each player in the national squad for a preseason, which had us working on a Saturday. All of us looked at him like he was mad. I can remember thinking at the time, 'This is a misprint. Who is this clown? I only do Monday to Friday in pre-season.' It's embarrassing to think how unprofessional we were. These days players do whatever it takes to get the best out of themselves and are often in on a Sunday morning doing rehab or having physio for bumps and bruises.

I cringe when I think of my physical stats and fitness test results at the time, and the fact that I thought they were any good. I saw myself as a professional rugby player, but I never asked myself why, when we were playing other fully professional sides, they were beating us easily. It wasn't because they were better rugby players, but because they were fitter and stronger than us. It really was that simple. It was no coincidence that Wales would always start games well and blow up 30 minutes before the end of a game. I am amazed none of us had worked out why! Unbelievable. Ignorance really was bliss. We didn't have a clue and we all had to be re-educated about what it took to be a professional.

I have always believed that Welsh rugby players are intuitively as good as anyone you will find in New Zealand or France, but the biggest change is that we have improved our physical approach to the game. We are as skilful, but now are also as fit and as strong as they are. Somebody such as Shane Williams may be the smallest player in Test match rugby, but he is probably one of the toughest, too. How good is Shane for world rugby, let alone Welsh rugby? He reminds us all that the game is still about great skills and great feet. He is proof, literally, that little things can make the biggest difference. I think he is a great role model for Welsh rugby, too. Think of how many Welsh youngsters will grow up wanting to play the game because they have watched Shane.

Steve always kept us on our toes and taught all of us that being a professional rugby player was a 24/7 occupation. He would bang home to us that we had decided to be professional rugby players and were playing for our country, and that it was a privilege, not a sacrifice, to do whatever was needed to be a success.

When I see some of the younger academy players coming through now, I see how things have changed in such a short space of time. We have teenagers who don't drink and who look after their bodies, living the life of professional sportsmen and women. They have to cope with the peer pressure of their friends probably going out enjoying themselves, knowing they cannot do the same. They simply cannot allow themselves to be distracted by outside influences. It's a great test of character and their desire to be professional rugby players, and I feel it shows the respect they have for the job they have chosen.

Nobody can have everything in life, and regional rugby in Wales now exposes those players who aren't living the life; those who haven't done the work or made the sacrifices simply don't make it. The days of those players who used to train like Tarzan and play like Jane have long gone, too. Rugby is a hard, physical game. There is nowhere to hide on the field and nobody can simply go through the motions, because they will be found out. Every player has to be motivated and driven and have a real hunger to succeed. Steve brought in that kind of mindset, which is now the norm and expected of players in Wales. Players these days train whenever they need to.

I can remember Steve talked about bringing in an alcohol breathalyser test for the morning after a Test match, which was something he had done at Canterbury. He didn't actually introduce one to the Wales set-up, but he did bring in ice-baths after a game, which, despite how much I despise them, I know do something to aid my recovery. He introduced computers, with every player getting his own personal laptop, and the idea of players doing their own PowerPoint presentations to the rest of the squad. We would be split into groups and have to give a talk to the rest of the group on a certain facet of the opposition's play or a topic about the game. All of this stuff was about being professional, although some of those early presentations weren't that great and the wrong clips would pop up half the time! It was carnage in the beginning, but players doing their own analysis meant we were not only learning about the game but also growing as individuals, not just as rugby players.

I remember Sir Clive Woodward calling the Welsh players 'scary' on the Lions tour to New Zealand in 2005 because we were all confident about saying our bit in team meetings and doing presentations to the rest of the squad. It was a major shift in Welsh rugby culture, as traditionally our players had been shy and reserved in that area because we felt inferior to the English or the Irish. That has all changed. Now we back our knowledge and experience of the game and have grown more confident because of the success we have had. Using laptops and players doing their own analysis or presentations is the norm in every Welsh regional academy today. How different it all is from when the game first went pro.

When I first started out, I just wanted to play rugby and would always wonder how a weights session would make me a better rugby player. I can remember older players doing the same. We had a good running culture at Llanelli, so that would be the basis of our fitness for the season. We were all creatures of habit back then and were afraid of anything new. Now the culture is completely different. Everybody is looking for a different way to give players an edge. I think the Welsh rugby public, who don't get a chance to see the average working week of a rugby player or what really goes on behind the scenes, would be astounded at the attention to detail that is part of the culture at home. Welsh rugby, which used to be so closed to new ideas, now embraces different sports and innovations that might improve performance, and that can only be healthy, provided they are based on logic and science. I have done yoga in a community hall, surrounded by pensioners, in a bid to improve my flexibility. I have done gymnastics and been taught by judo specialists how to get the upper hand at the tackle area. It's all about ideas, and keeping the mind fresh and being challenged. The older I have got, the more open-minded I have become to all of these things, but as a kid I probably would have called for the men in white coats if I had been told I would be doing this kind of stuff towards the end of my career. Now I know I have to improve every season and cannot afford to stand still. I know I will be left behind if I don't improve. What is good enough this year won't be good enough next year.

Rugby fitness used to be all about aerobic fitness – basically, how long you could run during a game. Now, it is much more power-based because the maxim is: win the collisions in a game, and you win the game. That means players do much more explosive fitness. The downside of this is the number of injuries in the game. More players than ever are having major knee and shoulder reconstructions. I have never had a major operation during my career and, touch wood, it will stay that way.

I know I have been very fortunate, but I have had my fair share of stitches, and was knocked spark out in France. I had my nose broken by Paul Moriarty, the former Scarlets coach, in a Welsh Cup final, with his famous swinging arm. I have done the ligaments in both of my ankles, broken my thumb twice and did the medial ligaments in my knee against Australia in an autumn Test at the Millennium Stadium. But I am one of the lucky ones and cannot grumble about my injury record.

Probably one of the reasons that I have been lucky with injury is that my playing weight isn't that much more than it would be if I weren't a rugby player. My muscle mass may be bigger and body fat level much lower, but my frame does carry my body weight naturally. Some players have to bulk up quite substantially to play in a certain position or role and they are much heavier than they would normally be, and that puts much more stress on their joints. The body can break down if the frame cannot carry the manufactured body weight.

I have nothing but admiration for Mark Jones, the Scarlets skipper, for the way he dealt with and battled his way back from two career-threatening knee injuries. He had two major knee reconstructions, one almost straight after the other, but he came back to play for the Scarlets and then for Wales. Amazing. He was out of rugby for a total of two years but was diligent about his rehab work and made it back. I don't know how he did it, and don't know if I could have done the same.

It's silly things that hit you when you are injured, like trying to make a cup of tea and moving back to the sofa when you are on crutches. How do you use the crutches and carry the tea at the same time? When a player makes a comeback like that, it shows how much they love the game and that they are made of special stuff. I have experienced a spell on the sidelines and it was not something I enjoyed at all. You aren't part of the team, have your own rehab and fitness schedule, and you feel like a complete outsider. Coming back from injury can be a lonely experience because the team – coaches and players – are all focused on the next game and you aren't part of it. I am not a great watcher of rugby, and sitting in the stands as a spectator while my teammates play is not something I enjoy. I don't feel part of the game. Although I am emotionally attached to what is happening, I have no control or any input into what is going on out on the field. It's bloody frustrating and I would usually rather be anywhere else.

The only physical issue I have is a long-standing problem with my back. There is nothing structurally wrong with it, but I do have to manage the odd back spasm. It is something I have had to deal with since I started playing. It means I have a very individual training programme devised just for me, where I don't do certain exercises and weights sessions or anything that puts pressure on my back. A lot of players, especially when they get older, carry the wear and tear of their career. I don't think there is a player around who doesn't have some problem he has to handle.

I manage my body very deliberately now and I have come to understand that more the older I have got. I have been educated to listen to my body and know when it's telling me I need a break or cannot do something. When I was younger, I would just plough on regardless, but now I know that's stupidity. One thing I have learnt is that prevention is better than cure. Gwen, my girlfriend, is a physio and she is always on my case about my posture, making sure I don't slump in front of the TV after I have been training. The natural reaction, when you are physically tired, is to put your feet up and relax, but that can be the worst thing to do. That's why physios and masseurs are now so commonplace – and worth their weight in gold for any rugby set-up. So many of them have looked after me and probably helped prolong my career.

I have no plans to retire from the game yet. I think I have a couple of good years left in the game, but I wonder how many players will play past the age of 30 in the future. I started out playing as a teenager, but most of the games I played earlier in my career were pretty sub-standard and nowhere near the physical examination they are these days. Rugby is now a collision sport and the demands on the body are extreme.

I have been lucky that I have been looked after by the Scarlets and the national set-up for the last few years and have been managed really well. I have learnt so much from watching how other players manage their bodies and working out what works for me.

The days of being flogged right up to the day of a game are now long gone. Players do the hard physical work earlier because we have learnt that tired players won't deliver the goods on the field on a weekend. It sounds ever so simple, but it wasn't appreciated during the early days of my career. Players cannot be emotionally or physically flat when they run out on a Saturday; they have to be excited, running onto the pitch. Warren Gatland, the current Wales coach, has a really good feel for where his players are and isn't afraid to cut short or change the working week if he can see the squad isn't in a good place.

One of the physical areas I have had to improve during my career is my flexibility and mobility. My physio at Clermont in France couldn't believe how bad I was in those two areas. I can remember him doing some work on my body and shaking his head in bemusement, then getting the other physios and players to come in and look at me. They were all talking in French. I felt like an absolute freak. I did a lot of stretching and different kinds of mobility exercises every week in France.

French rugby was also an eye-opener when it came to the working week. The team run on the day before the game was very different from what I had experienced at the Scarlets. At Clermont, it was a 35-minute session, done flat-out and at game intensity. Warren Gatland would introduce the same style of approach for every session when he took over as Wales coach. Previously, team runs had been just be a gentle run-out and a reminder about the game plan and the moves and tactics we were going to use for a match. There was no rush or intensity, and the focus was on getting things right. The working week in France was also much, much shorter than what I had been used to in Wales. We had to travel long distances on the team coach, sometimes leaving Clermont on a Thursday, with a seven- or eight-hour coach journey ahead, to play on a Saturday. The weights culture in France was also very different from what I was used to. We'd do weights in Clermont, but most French clubs didn't at all. Horey would always send me my weight programmes by email, though, which allowed me to do specific Welsh training throughout the season while I was abroad.

I do miss the old-fashioned team-bonding sessions. Team-building exercises, like windsurfing or whatever, have never done anything for me. It's a nice day out, but not much more than that. I still believe a couple of beers, within reason, is the best way to get to know your teammates. It's a chance to get away from the pressures and emotions of a game and to just enjoy each other's company. I know sides still target times in a season for a good get-together, but they are few and far between these days. The best team-bonding now is playing and winning together. That's why we play the game, after all.

I can remember Johno once introducing 'Sledging Tuesday', as his idea of a kind of team-bonding during a training session with Wales. As a typical Aussie, Johno loves the banter and the trash talk and he told the whole squad they could sledge as much as they wanted during this particular training session. To say it got out of hand would be an understatement. Ceri Sweeney absolutely tore Hal Luscombe verbally to bits on the field and it got, shall we say, very tasty. Johno had to stop 'Sledging Tuesday' after only an hour because things had gone too far. Brilliant.

The night before a game every player has his own routine. If we are based at the team hotel or away from home, it usually means watching a film in the team room or, if I am with Wales, some of us will watch the Wales Under-20s on TV. Some players do have routines they always like to follow, but I am not superstitious and don't have any particular habits I follow religiously. Some players do, but I usually like to watch a game of rugby or rugby league on TV the night before a game. Some of the boys will be on their phones and laptops, too, but it is all pretty calm.

Playing rugby is now our job and we all know what is required from us the following day. I try not to get caught up in all the emotion and hype surrounding the game and like to stay calm, but I do run through the moves I will need in a game in my head. I remind myself that Rob Howley, the attack coach at Wales, wants a good mix of passing, running and kicking in my game, so I run through what my role is on the pitch. I don't have any problems sleeping before a game. I seem to have become more excited, rather than nervous, about playing these days.

In my opinion, very few people really appreciate how far Welsh rugby has come in such a short space of time. Welsh sides would regularly be on the end of some big beatings on the international and European stage, but that doesn't happen any more. We aren't a big country population-wise, and aren't rich, but that hasn't stopped us competing with England and France in recent times. Our two Grand Slams prove that. We now have world-class facilities and stadiums, and an academy structure that produces professional rugby players. Some of the best coaches in the world have come to Wales and I have been lucky enough to work with them. The national side and the regional sides are all good rugby teams now.

Regional rugby has kept every professional player hungry and on his toes. Players know just being a regional player isn't good enough – they have to have ambitions to be the best in Wales, then the best in the world. That is the way it should be. There was a time when Welsh rugby rewarded mediocrity, but not any more.

As I have got older, I have learnt how to handle the job of being a professional player. With the season now about ten months, it is impossible to peak every week for every game. There isn't a player who can do it. It's impossible. I have learnt to manage my season, and I know when I need a break from the game and when I need to get away completely so that I come back mentally fresh and stimulated. That is something that has come through experience, and only towards the end of my career. I hate predictability; the 'it's weights for half an hour now, then lunch and then sprints' – knowing when I will be doing it every day or every week. I need spontaneity and to be challenged. There is nothing worse for a rugby player than just going through the motions and not being stimulated. I hate dull training sessions and not being challenged more and more. I hate doing anything for the sake of just doing it; there has to be a purpose and a quantifiable goal to achieve. I want there to be a purpose for everything and to know I am becoming a better player or getting a better understanding of the game. I know I have to eat the right things, do my weights sessions and look after my body, but it's the rugby sessions that are now key for every player. You don't want to be hanging around on the pitch; you just want to get down to work. That is my office and is where I do my job.

There is no doubt that my career has coincided with the most challenging and traumatic period in the history of Welsh rugby. I made my debut when Wales were hammered by South Africa in

1998. Everybody thought Wales were finished as a major force. But I have seen Welsh rugby adapt and finally get to grips with the professional game. I have been lucky enough to win two Grand Slams and, when I retire, Welsh rugby will be in a much better place than it was when I started my career. The 'as long as we beat the English' mindset has finally gone. Now, we are a competitive rugby nation again and, I believe, can look any major rugby country in the eye and have a chance of beating them on a rugby field.

CHAPTER 9

COMING HOME – THE SCARLETS AND THE BLUES

West is best.

– Ray Gravell, Scarlets, Wales and Lions rugby legend

The decision to return home to Wales after two years in France was easy to make. Where I would play was the difficult question for me. It was a simple shoot-out between the Scarlets, my spiritual home, and the Blues. Lyn Jones, then Ospreys coach, had spoken to me about joining him at the Liberty Stadium, and that was very flattering, but, as a former Scarlet, it was just a bit too close to the bone for me.

I'd decided to leave Clermont and not take up my option for a third year in France because I wanted to be in the best possible nick for the 2007 World Cup. Wales had a maturing team and I wanted to make sure I was at my physical and mental peak for the tournament. Rugby in France can be a gruelling slog and playing the Top 14 means an incredibly long season. It does eventually take its toll mentally, as well as physically.

While I had loved my time in French rugby, it had been very demanding in terms of travelling back and forth to Wales for international duty. The endless flights and the number of planes

I had to catch to get to Cardiff had become something I could do without. I had returned for my second season with Clermont after the disappointment of the Lions tour to New Zealand on my shoulders and was back playing rugby pretty soon afterwards. I hadn't had a pre-season, something I know that I need, so was thrown straight back into the demands of the Top 14. My second season in France was a really tough one; I had picked up a couple of niggling injuries and realised something had to give.

People have said I didn't play as well in my second season in France, but I don't really agree with that. My problem was recovering from the Lions tour. The lack of a decent pre-season meant my fitness wasn't as good as it should have been. The thought of a third season with six- or seven-hour bus journeys travelling back to Clermont after an away game, with the endless coffee and cigarette breaks, then getting home to bed at four or five o'clock in the morning, had started to take its toll. The World Cup in France the following season, though, was also a big factor in my decision to return to Wales.

Clermont wanted me to stay, and made me a very good offer for a third season, but I just knew that with the World Cup on the horizon it would mean a lot of rugby with Wales and with Clermont. They were paying my wages and, quite rightly, would want me to play every game for them in the French Championship. I just knew that it would be unrealistic. The thought of being caught in the middle, between Wales and Clermont, wasn't something I wanted. I had to make a decision and take control of the situation.

In the end, it was a no-brainer, really. I wanted to return to Wales, where you are spoilt and looked after, and where every player can prepare for Test match rugby in a controlled environment. Like I say, the decision to return may have been easy, but deciding where I wanted to play wasn't.

David Young, the Blues coach and a former Wales captain, was somebody I had played alongside in the international set-up and is someone, as a coach and a bloke, for whom I have the highest regard. He made it very clear he wanted me to join the Arms Park and did a great job of selling the impressive vision he has for the Blues to me. He had put together an excellent squad and set-up at the Blues, but it was his ambition for the place that was spellbinding. Dai had been through some really tough times at the Blues, but he had stuck to his principles and his vision and had come out the other side, and now he was starting to see his plan come to fruition. As a player, you could only be impressed by a coach like that, and all his players had only good things to say about him. He was a tough cookie and had always put himself in the firing line when things weren't going well, protecting his team, and that is all you want as a player.

The Scarlets, on the other hand, meant so much to me and had given me everything in rugby. There was a big emotional pull for me to return there, and they had big plans in the pipeline for a new state-of-the-art stadium.

On the surface, it should have been a simple decision for me, but it wasn't, because I was wary of just slipping back into the same old comfort zone and routine with the Scarlets. It was that old saying, 'Never go back.' I was also very aware of not just making the easy decision and signing for the Scarlets because I felt I was supposed to. The pull of the Blues and the chance to try something new was very real.

I had made a tough decision to leave the Scarlets when I signed for Clermont and that had proved to be a good decision for me as a player and a person. It had pushed me out of my comfort zone and forced me to grow up. The Blues were also a side going places and had superb new training facilities in the pipeline, and on the horizon there was the prospect of playing in a new stadium. Dai had really impressed me with how he had begun to build something real in the Welsh capital and the ambitions he had to put the Blues at the top of European rugby.

I know I tested the patience of everybody at both regions while they waited for my decision and my solicitor and manager, Duncan

Sandlant, too, had the patience of a saint as I tried to make up my mind. We are close friends and I am delighted to see his company, Point Sports Management, doing well. He represents some of the bigger names in world rugby and has worked hard for his success. The pros and cons list came out again, as I tried to decide where I should play my rugby back in Wales. My heart was telling me the Scarlets, but my head was telling me the Blues.

Looking back, I am not proud of how I handled the whole situation, but the Blues were brilliant to me. I had actually given my word to Dai that I would join him at the Arms Park. Legally, my word was binding and, in principle, the Blues held all the aces and could have taken me to court and forced me to play for them. If they'd wanted, I could be playing for the Blues now. I didn't have a leg to stand on and can only thank the club for being so understanding. But it was a long telephone conversation with Simon Easterby, the Scarlets captain, that changed my mind. He knew I was wavering and that I was leaning towards the Blues, and also that I would be wary of signing for the Scarlets because that was what everybody expected me to do. Easters was in Wales and I was in France and during that long phone conversation he convinced me I should return to my beloved Scarlets.

Si may be a Yorkshireman who has played for Ireland, but his feeling and passion for the Scarlets is as strong as, if not stronger than any Welshman's. Just like Rupert Moon and Tony Copsey, who are both from outside Wales, the place is now in his blood and it means everything to him. He is a Scarlet through and through and was incredibly positive about the future at the Scarlets and what could be achieved. We had both been part of sides that had done well in Europe and he believed the Scarlets could scale those heights again. He also talked about the responsibility of playing for the Scarlets and of rugby in the region, and his words really hit a chord with me. I had grown up as a man and a player at Stradey and it had given me everything. I wouldn't have achieved half of what I have achieved in the game without the support I was given there. I had played in Heineken Cup quarter-finals and semi-finals and won the Celtic League title with the Scarlets. I had also grown up with the likes of Dwayne Peel, Mark Jones and Barry Davies, and playing alongside them did excite me. In the end, I felt I had a duty to return there and to sign for the Scarlets.

Once I had finally made the decision to return to Stradey, it meant I had to tell Dai and the hierarchy at the Blues that I had done a U-turn. It wasn't a conversation I was looking forward to. I rang Dai and asked to meet him face-to-face. I wanted to fly in from France to meet him in Cardiff and explain my decision. I told him I had changed my mind and apologised for mucking him around, but Dai was as good as gold and accepted my decision, saying there was no need to fly home. Peter Thomas, the Blues chairman, was also very understanding. I have nothing but respect for the way they handled my situation. I knew I had let them down and led them up the garden path, and had put everybody in a difficult situation.

I actually saw Dai a few months later when I was on Wales duty at the WRU's training base at the Vale of Glamorgan. He walked around the corner towards me and my heart sank because I knew I had let him down in a big way. He shook my hand and, quick as a flash, in his deadpan way, he said, 'Thanks for nearly getting me the sack, Steve.' Only the glint in his eye and the half-smile across his face gave him away.

What Dai has done with the Blues has proved what a good coach he is and I couldn't be happier for him. The Blues are now a real force to be reckoned with. You don't win the Anglo-Welsh Cup and reach a Heineken Cup semi-final if you aren't. He had outlined what he wanted to achieve when we were in talks and he has done most of it. I have no doubt the Blues will go from strength to strength with him in charge.

I have been asked if I have regrets, because the Scarlets are now in a rebuilding phase, but I don't do regrets. I made my decision and I am happy with it.

My first season back at Stradey Park was a joy. Phil Davies had taken over from Gareth Jenkins, who was now with Wales, and he had made a real impact. Phil's attention to detail and his work ethic are legendary. He was very different from Gareth and was very much in the mould of the modern high-tech coach. I picked up where I left off with Peely, and it was great to work in tandem with him again. We played a great brand of attacking rugby and, I would like to think, stuck to the Scarlets' philosophy and principles about the game. We beat Toulouse in Toulouse in the Heineken Cup and surprised everyone in Europe. Most people would have expected the Scarlets to come a real cropper against one of the genuine powerhouses of European rugby, and we nearly did. We were hanging at half-time after Toulouse had run us off our feet with a breathtaking brand of rugby, but we did the same in the second half. With both sides enjoying a beautiful December afternoon in France, with the sun on our backs, we played some great attacking rugby. We may have been down 31–10 at the break, but nobody was talking about a damage-limitation exercise or anything like that at half-time. We had beaten them 20–19 at Stradey the previous week and were confident we could match them, and we did exactly that.

Wing Darren Daniel and full-back Barry Davies both crossed for tries before Darren got his second of the match when Cedric Heyman fumbled a kick. Regan King then carved his way through the Toulouse defence for Nathan Thomas to score the winning try. I had played Toulouse in Toulouse twice with Clermont and had been on the losing side both times, but we had emerged with a 41–34 win. We were the first side to beat them on their own patch since 2000 and it gave us all such a boost of confidence.

We would finish unbeaten in our Pool and I still believe that win was our best victory as a regional side. We then knocked out the reigning champions, Munster, in one of those great European nights at Stradey. The place always had a real magic about it when European rugby was the order of the day, with the floodlights and a sell-out crowd. It was an intimidating venue for any visiting side and we brought a real intensity and drive to everything we did. Munster were without skipper Paul O'Connell, but we were in control for most of the game and we soon secured a third semi-final place.

Leicester in the Walkers Stadium was where our dream of finally winning the Heineken Cup ended. It was almost a case of déjà vu, but we were well beaten 33–17 by the Tigers in the Midlands. They pretty much bullied us out of the game and really frustrated us. We couldn't really get our attacking game, which had served us so well up until then, going at all. But still I felt my decision to come back to the Scarlets had been vindicated.

CHAPTER 10

THE SCIENCE OF
THE FLY-HALF

Rugby is a thinking man's game.

– *Carwyn James, legendary Llanelli and
British and Irish Lions coach*

The Wales number 10 jersey has gained a mythical, almost romantic place in Welsh life and culture, let alone rugby. It is up there with the Brazil number 10 shirt in football when it comes to tradition, status and history. It has been a huge honour to wear a shirt that has been worn by so many great players, but if you thought too long and hard about them all you wouldn't get out of bed, let alone onto the pitch.

Cliff Morgan, David Watkins, Barry John, Phil Bennett and Jonathan Davies are all legendary Welsh outside-halfs. They conjure up all sorts of romantic images and have provided the legacy for the shirt I have been privileged to wear. The Welsh fly-half does have a certain place in the nation's psyche – and it is usually in the image of a fleet-footed wizard ghosting through defences and dancing his way to the try line.

I would never be arrogant enough to claim I am in the same mould as them. I am not. I will never be known as a dancing number 10 or anything like that. I am much more in the mould of another great Welsh fly-half, Neil Jenkins, or England's World Cup winner, Jonny Wilkinson. All of us are the eyes and ears of any side we play for and it is our job to implement the game plan of the team on the field and to get the very best out of the players around us.

While the role and the principles of a fly-half appear very similar to what they have always been, they have changed out of sight since I started playing. I would go even further than that and say that the technical aspects of rugby have changed the position even more dramatically over the last five years. The role and principles of a fly-half, even for a great player such as Dan Carter of the All Blacks, or Juan Martín Hernández of Argentina, are very similar in the modern game. We all have our own strengths and weaknesses. Players like Carter or Matt Giteau are renowned for being great runners with the ball in hand, while the likes of Wilkinson and South Africa's Morne Steyn are known for their excellent kicking games. But overall the fly-half role is very similar for all of us and our primary job is to choose the right option, reward our forwards for their hard work and get the best out of the talent outside us. A good fly-half recognises the strengths of his own team and tries to expose the weaknesses of the opposition. We are the brains, if you like, or the facilitators for the team. We have to see what is happening on the field and interpret it. Then, while chaos reigns around us, we have to make the right decisions at the right time. It sounds simple, but when you have a second to make the right decision, it's not.

What makes a good outside-half? Well, how long is a piece of string? The fly-half's role in the modern game is to implement the game plan of the coaches. Rugby has always been a strategic game, even in the amateur days. That hasn't changed, but it has become more structured and technical in the pro era. Tactically, it is miles away from the game I first started playing and the fly-half role, which was so instinctive, has become more scientific.

In my early days, I was told to just go out and play and react to the situation in front of me. Simply play what was in front of me.

Now that the analysis of every player and team is so detailed, it would be naive to think that is possible. It's all about picking up on a weakness in the opposition, coming up with a strategy to expose that weakness and then trying to implement that strategy during the game. It's all about knowing the traits of a particular player and team and using them for your benefit. Now, I have to take the team through five or six phases before the play breaks up and I have the opportunity to react to what is in front of me.

The basics of every game plan for every number 10 are pretty simple. You have an agreed number of devised moves from scrums, lineout and kick-offs. Then, within those devised moves, there are a certain number of options that a fly-half has to call and use, as he sees fit, for the team. It's a bit like a game of chess. You may have a particular move that has been designed to play to your strengths or to expose the opposition's weaknesses. It's pretty simple stuff, but the biggest thing is that you are the decision-maker on the field. It's the number 10's job to make the right call, take the right option and do it at the right time. Then it's all about execution and making it happen on the field. I don't think that has changed much over the years. It's just the time and space to work in that has almost disappeared!

You also have to recognise the strengths you have and want to play to in your own team, and the weaknesses you may have to mask for your side. You have to understand a teammate's ability and his mental strengths. After a game, if I get a chance, I ask the opposition coach what their game plan was against the side I was playing in. I always enjoyed picking Pat Howard's brain after a game. I find it fascinating to hear what they had devised and what plan they were trying to execute against us. I usually know when it has worked, and sometimes I am surprised by what I hear, but I always learn something from that process. It gives me a chance to see how a fresh pair of eyes views my side's strengths and weaknesses.

There are, for me, some key areas you have to understand about the role of the outside-half in the professional game. The fly-half is the face of every team. He is the general on the field. He is the player everybody in the side looks to and he has to relish that responsibility. The role has become more and more like that of a quarterback in American football.

If there are qualities a good number 10 needs, I would say they are composure, calmness and the ability to communicate on the field. You have to be very vocal and issue instructions and directions while the game goes on around you. There is limited time for debate and your teammates have to trust you to make the right decisions. You need to be able to handle pressure and offer answers to the questions being posed on the pitch. Every fly-half has to have utter belief in his ability and be mentally tough. You always have to back yourself at key moments and never shrink when the pressure or spotlight falls on you. Why? Because it's usually the fly-half, as the key decision-maker for the team, who gets the blame if his side doesn't perform or win. Every fly-half has to have absolute confidence in his own ability and the game plan he has to implement, and know his preparation is spot on.

The fly-half is the energiser of every team. You always have to be positive about what is going on in the game because you cannot have teammates looking at you and seeing negative body language or indecision or lack of control. You have to be so focused on what you are trying to achieve, and be calm and level-headed throughout the game. I am not afraid to say that has been the biggest challenge for me over the years. Though age and experience have helped, I did used to get very emotional on the pitch and carried away with what was happening in a game. Playing at number 10 is about communication, faith and vision. Allowing the red mist to engulf you only clouds your decision-making on the field.

I still believe leading your side's attack is the primary role of every fly-half. Having the ability to unlock the opposition's defence is the biggest challenge for every number 10, at whatever level you play the game. It is still possible, even in the claustrophobic world of Test match rugby, to find space on the field. Defences may be better than they ever have been, more disciplined and more aggressive, but it is still impossible for 15 players to defend every blade of grass on a rugby pitch. I always try to remember that when I am in a tight match, because sometimes you can become obsessed with the close-quarter arm-wrestle and banging away at the same point in the opponent's defence when there could be space out wide. Whether you are facing a blitz defence, a drift defence or a side that doesn't commit numbers to the tackle area, it's down to the number 10 to see and find the space on the field.

While I have said the fly-half has to be the eyes of his team, he also has to be the ears, and listen to the players outside him. There is so much heavy traffic in the professional game, and if your team is getting quick ball and is on the front foot you need voices outside you to make the call if they have spotted a weakness in the defensive line. For this to happen, you need rugby-intelligent players outside you who can read what is happening in front of them. You need your teammates to give you the correct information at the right time to make the right call. The likes of Regan King, Tom Shanklin and Brian O'Driscoll are all excellent at this. Again, playing at number 10 is about communication, faith and vision.

The golden rule for every fly-half is never to take the ball stationary, and the mantra is a simple: RUN . . . CATCH . . . PASS. Always take the ball on the move. Scott Johnson taught me another rule for every fly-half, and it is one that I still adhere to. It's pretty simple, but the number 10 has to bring his centres onto the ball and make sure they finish ahead of him when he has passed them the ball. That means you stay alive in the game, have the option of a double-touch and don't have to work to get back behind the ball. Also, the further you pass the ball back, the easier you make life for the opposition defence, and the more time they have to recover and manage your attack. As a general rule, the way I like to play is to have my 12 and 13 running in a line with me and to have my wings and full-back ready to come in, wherever they want, as a second wave of attackers. I believe it's a good rule for any fly-half to remember.

The French approach, from my time with Clermont, was very different. They liked their backs to be physical, play with real depth and come onto the ball at real pace. I have probably learnt more about attacking play in France than anywhere else. The fly-half is told he has to be an attacking threat in France and he has to be able to play with varied width, which keeps the defence constantly thinking and guessing about what is going to happen next. While the rest of the backs were always aligned very deep, I was taught to play flat and told I had to play in the face of the opposition defence and put them under as much pressure as possible. To do that, you need quick hands and I certainly developed them in France. This philosophy was the absolute opposite to what we adopted in Wales at the time. The Welsh back line played much flatter compared with any back-liners in France.

The ability to pass, with speed and precision, is absolutely vital for every fly-half. You have to be accurate and have the ability to distribute off both hands; the weight and speed of the pass can be the difference between scoring a try and butchering a try-scoring opportunity and throwing an interception pass, which could lead to the opposition racing away and scoring a try. It is all about doing your job, timing and fixing your opposite number and getting the ball to your centres as early as possible. Sometimes you do throw a pass blind in a set move, hoping and having faith that a teammate will be in the correct space at the correct time and is alive to what you are going to do. If it works, you look like a genius. If it doesn't, you look like a fool – and have some major issues!

The real key for every outside-half is that you have to take the ball early. You need to get the ball in your hands as soon as possible. It sounds simple, but never let the ball come to you and cradle it in your chest. That is why you see most number 10s putting their hands in the direction from which they expect the ball to come to them. No fly-half worth his salt has his hands by his sides, and when he has caught the ball he always keeps it in both hands.

I know this sounds basic, but any budding fly-halfs who can master this skill will give themselves, and also their teammates, so much more time on the field. By the same token, holding the ball for too long eats into your teammates' space and time and allows the defence to manage any threat you pose. The 'blitz' defence has made holding onto the ball too long absolutely fatal. The blitz calling card of good defensive line speed and getting 'man and ball' with a big hit is the defensive side's way of telling you 'too slow and too predictable'.

I am now in the twilight of my career, and when I look back at some of my performances in my early days, I am embarrassed by some of the things I used to do on the field. I know it's a bit of a cliché, but you do learn more, and your learning curve is sharper, when you lose games. Defeat forces you to reflect, reassess and then review your game. I still feel I am learning about my role and the game; I wish I had started my career with all the knowledge I have towards the end of it. I suppose every athlete feels the same.

The biggest challenge I have faced throughout my career as a fly-half has been controlling my emotions. I always used to want to get stuck in and do my bit for the team and carry the ball, make my tackles, hit rucks and make my contribution at the contact area. I know it is completely at odds with the traditional view of a Welsh number 10, but it was how I wanted to play and the style that suited me. When I was younger, I was always pumped up for every game, played with aggressive body language and, if the red mist descended on me during a game, I would play the game with blinkers on. Of course, it doesn't help me to do my job if my thought process is clouded with emotion. Some players, like Serge Betsen, are very good at keeping you out of the game after tackling you by any means possible. Serge would lie or sit on you, and keep you out of the next phase of play so you could not dictate what happened next.

As I have got older, I have learnt what my role is for the team and there is no point, as the fly-half, being stuck out of position at the bottom of a ruck. As the fly-half, I cannot afford to be out of position and can have more influence on a game in the fly-half position. As I said earlier, I am the eyes of the side.

These days a good defence is paramount, and a major part of the working week is devoted to it. It is the very basic foundation of every side's approach to the game. Defences are so well organised and can suffocate any team's attacking ability. The fly-half has to be able to defend and has to make his tackles – that is a given now. Jenks was probably the first Welsh fly-half to really understand and define the defensive role of the number 10. Jonny Wilkinson is another who prides himself on this facet of the game and probably took it to another level.

The number 10 channel on the field is now where most teams attack, and there is a lot of heavy traffic in front of you. The first thing many teams do is test the fly-half's defence to see if he is really up for the physical battle. That is why it's so important you don't shirk your duties here and are as aggressive as possible. If you don't make your tackles or slip off a few early on, they will keep on coming and you will be in for a long afternoon. The last thing you want to be seen as is a defensive liability or a weak link in the chain, because it throws your defensive line into chaos. Your teammates need to know they can trust you to play your part in defence, and that allows them to focus on *their* role in defence.

Some teams now move their fly-half out of the firing line to save him doing all the donkey work in defence and put him somewhere else in the defensive line. He will then come back into the 10 spot for attacking plays. That means he is fresh, clear-headed and doesn't get beaten up and battered by all the physical stuff. That is why it's so easy to compare the fly-half role to that of the quarter-back in the NFL, where every other player's job is to protect him and his contribution to the team. As I get older, I have to say, I like this idea more and more!

The kicking game is where every fly-half knows he will be judged and it is a constant challenge. Kicking is all about the hours spent on the training field. There are no short cuts. The importance of a fly-half's kicking game cannot be underestimated, as it is vital to him and his team. You have to master the kicking game and need a wide range of kicks in your armoury. Defensive kicks, chip kicks, grubber kicks, cross kicks, spiral kicks, drop punts and now even banana kicks are all expected to be part of your game. That's before we even talk about drop kicks and goal kicks. This probably hasn't changed at all down the years; the biggest difference nowadays in the professional game is that every fly-half's kicking success is measured and the percentages of successful kicks have soared. A fly-half now has to be able to kick on the run; and you cannot just sit back and admire your work. It is no good being stationary. You have to keep moving and make sure you are always an attacking threat. No fly-half worth his salt can sit back and admire his work and become a statue after he has kicked. That's why kicking on the run has become so important. It means you are still an attacking threat to the opposition. If you are stationary, you will have made the defence's life easier than you should have. A good kick, as every coach will tell you, is only as good as the chase, and there is nothing worse than a good kick and a poor chase. Having said that, how many times have you seen a poorly executed kick saved by a good chase?

Goal-kicking has always been important. It has always been measured by how many you convert and how many you miss. Pretty obvious, and it hasn't changed at all over the years. Every goal-kicker, when he walks off at the final whistle, knows how well, or how badly, he has done in this facet of the game. What has changed is that his success or failure at kicking out of hand has now been measured, too. Kicking out of hand has always been important, but its accuracy, distance and execution has made it more so in the modern game. Every team now has more than one kicking option and more than one player who can kick a ball. The rule is simple: the more kicking options you have, the more dangerous you are as a side.

Wales are blessed with a lot of players who can kick, and it has become a real bonus for us in a game. Neil Jenkins always says the fact we have so many good kickers puts the full-back and wings we play against under pressure. It means they don't know where the ball is going to come from, and it makes it difficult to read our kicking strategy. It also means their primary focus is on managing that threat rather than becoming an attacking threat in their own right.

All the backs are now expected to be skilled in this area of the game. If your fly-half is the only kicker in the team, it makes life so easy for the opposition back three – full-back and wings – because they know there is a good chance when you get the ball that you are going to kick. It also means they only have one kicker to mark up during a game. It means they can nullify your kicking game, in attack or defence, and take an element of your game away from you.

Kicking has traditionally been seen as mainly a defensive action but is now viewed as a real attacking weapon. It used to be all about gaining field position, the up-and-under, but now when you see space the correct kick and execution can expose a defence and create havoc.

The attacking cross kick, which was perfected in rugby league, is another weapon in a fly-half's armoury and it catches any side using the blitz defence. A good grubber kick or chip kick does the same. It can catch a defence flat-footed and forces them to turn, and so puts you on the front foot.

I have always found goal-kicking a major challenge throughout my career and I don't expect that to ever change. Different countries play with different makes of rugby ball and that means each ball has a different sweet spot. One make of rugby ball travels through the air in a very different way from another. Some countries, like France, use different air pressure in their balls. The French, for whatever reason, like a softer ball and don't pump it up as much as the rest of Europe. All of these things have to be taken into account wherever you play around the world. I know, and totally appreciate, that every fly-half will be remembered for his success as a goal-kicker. It comes with the territory, and with the job. But the mental calmness and focus required for a penalty or conversion is so at odds with the physical aspect of the game. It's a major challenge to find that calmness. Take, for example, the long-range penalty I missed with the last kick of the game against Ireland in the final game of the 2009 Six Nations. It was a major challenge for me. I had just played 80 minutes of a brutally physical game, my adrenaline was pumping, I was carrying the bumps and bruises of the game and then I had to focus on a penalty kick to seal victory. All the time, I knew all the supporters in the stands at the Millennium Stadium, who were fresh and had enjoyed a great game of rugby, were praying I would kick the points. I didn't strike the ball that badly, but the distance beat me. It was at the edge of my range of kicking, but I had converted a kick earlier from the same distance. But kicking when you are fresh at the start of a game, compared with kicking at the end, requires a completely different mental focus.

My body is fatigued towards the end of a game and that is when my mental routine comes into play. I cannot tell you how lucky I am to have had somebody like Jenks around while I have been playing. He is just tremendous and I am always picking his brains. He is big on routine, practice and finding what works for you as a kicker. He always challenges me and throws new ideas at me. He has a great feel for where a kicker is mentally. But goal-kickers do remember the kicks they missed rather than the ones that went over.

Ronan O'Gara told me on the 2009 Lions tour that he still lives with the kicks he missed in Munster's first Heineken Cup final against Northampton Saints at Twickenham in 2000. Those disappointments are the ones that drive you on and the experiences that make you the player you are. Goal-kicking is a hell of a challenge, but is one I welcome and that excites me. When I look back, I have had kicks to win the Welsh League with the Scarlets, to draw a Test for the Lions and to win a Triple Crown against Ireland, which I missed. The silence of kicking practice has become something I really enjoy and look forward to nowadays. It's just me and my thoughts. There is no mobile phone, just a ball and some rugby posts and a chance to escape from everything. It's a bit like being a fisherman. It gives me time to myself and time to think about the game on the horizon, or to just blank everything out and search for the perfect kick.

Goal-kicking, like a match, can be so unpredictable. I can kick everything in training and watch every ball sail through the posts, then be slightly out of sync the next day and struggle to find my rhythm. There is no obvious reason for it. Kicking is a great battle.

I cannot state how important it is for the team for a good fly-half to be very vocal. It is expected that anybody who wears the number 10 jersey can direct operations and isn't afraid to tell his teammates what to do or when to do it. Your pack of forwards are usually locked in combat with the opposition and need directions and to be told what is happening around them. The fly-half has to be able to see the whole picture and be confident enough to demand the ball at the correct time when he sees a chink in the opposition's armour. That doesn't mean I have to shout and scream at everybody, because some players know their role inside out, but others need to be told when they have broken a pattern of play agreed before the game. Some players know instinctively what they have to do and others need to be managed. The fly-half's job is to make sure all the great work of the forwards doesn't go to waste, and to pick the right time to attack a certain part of the defensive line or part of the field.

When I first established myself in the Wales side, it was a very hard thing for the players to tell one another when they had done something wrong. We were probably too nice to each other. Now we have a culture where players tell each other home truths for the good of the team. Every side needs that. It requires a certain kind of confidence to tell a teammate that he isn't pulling his weight, but it is absolutely vital for any side's success that it happens. I can remember the first time Dwayne Peel, as a young player starting at the time, started to bark at me during a game. Peely had been pretty quiet on the field up until a Scarlets game against Bourgoin in the Heineken Cup, but it all changed during that game. It's no surprise he was quiet, because he had Scott Quinnell at number 8 and myself at number 10. He was getting on my case during the game and I just turned around to him and said, 'Concentrate on your own game.' It was the first time he had showed he was comfortable telling me, an older player, the truth. Peely had arrived. Young players do find it hard to be honest with each other, but you have to appreciate the opinions of others because they may see something you haven't seen on the field.

I wouldn't call myself a perfectionist, but I always want to improve and better myself and play the perfect game. I know that will never happen. It's like a dog chasing its tail, but that is what I – and I am sure every sportsperson – strive for when I take the field. It is what I am aiming for and the day I lose the desire to play the perfect game is when I knock it on the head.

I always know I can improve. I don't think there is a game I have played where I haven't seen something I could have improved on or an error that I need to eradicate from my game. The only thing that eases that is when I have been part of a winning team. Even now it's a massive high to come off a field having won a game. I cannot really explain what a buzz and adrenaline rush it is to win – and it's even better when it's a big game against a big side. It's an incredible feeling. I am one of the lucky ones who get to experience it.

Over the last few years, I have appreciated that keeping calm and being able to analyse what is going on around me, and what the opposition are doing, is key to being a good fly-half. And I would like to think my performances have become more and more influential as I have got older because of that.

STEPHEN JONES: GOAL-KICKING – 2006–9

Regional

	2006–07	2007–08	2008–09
Attempted	106	55	102
Converted	76	42	79
Missed	30	13	23
Efficiency (per cent)	72	76	77

International

	2006–07	2007–08	2008–09	Lions
Attempted	36	24	31	33
Converted	26	19	20	25
Missed	10	5	11	8
Efficiency (per cent)	72	79	65	76

Total

	2006–07	2007–08	2008–09
Attempted	142	79	166
Converted	102	61	124
Missed	40	18	42
Efficiency (per cent)	72	77	75

CHAPTER 11

CAPTAINCY

> The ultimate measure of a man is not where he stands
> in moments of comfort, but where he stands at times of
> challenges and controversy.
>
> – *Martin Luther King, American civil rights leader*

Being made captain of your country is the greatest honour for any sportsperson, but for me it brought about the lowest point of my whole career. You learn to expect the highs and lows of sport, but some of the lows really hurt you personally.

I had just captained my country for the first time and we had been beaten by a record 43–9 by an England second-string at the Millennium Stadium. It wasn't supposed to have been like that at all. I got back to the team hotel, jumped in a cab on my own and headed off to meet Mark Jones, my Wales and Scarlets teammate, and his wife in Cardiff Bay. I was looking for answers, and looking for them in bottles of beer. Stupid. I didn't find any, but I kept looking for them in the same way for the rest of the night. I had never been that low or out of sorts because of rugby. All sorts of things were going through my mind. There I was, the captain of Wales, in a Cardiff nightclub in the early hours of the morning, a broken man. I was totally oblivious to anybody around me or of anything being said to me by passers-by. I was wrapped up in my own thoughts and disappointment. It was supposed to be the proudest day of my career, but I felt I had let down a lot of people, including myself. It wasn't good enough. The night disappeared in a blur.

That was the first and last time I reacted so badly and became so absorbed in my own emotions about a defeat. The despair of that defeat has subsided, but it still remains, to this day, the biggest disappointment of my career.

England had thumped us during one of the warm-up games before the 2003 World Cup in Australia – an England second-string had come to our home and run riot. It was the worst feeling I have ever had after a rugby game. We had worked harder physically than ever in the build-up to that game and come away with nothing. There was no reward for all the effort we had put in.

Steve Hansen had decided the whole squad were physically off the pace and that we needed to be blasted physically in training. We hadn't done any rugby in the build-up to the game and all the players had been put through the mill physically because the coaches had decided we had to be fitter, stronger and faster for the World Cup campaign ahead of us. They had blasted us in the week before the England game; I had never worked as hard physically in my life. Every day was like a gruelling physical examination where we were pushed to our very physical and mental extremes. It was physical punishment of the most brutal kind. We had hardly seen a rugby ball and paid the price with defeat.

My first taste of captaincy had come about because of Steve's decision to pick four co-captains for the 2003 summer tour to New Zealand and Australia. It caused quite an uproar at the time. Steve explained his rationale behind the move, and made it clear he felt we lacked leadership in the squad and wanted to see if we had any natural leaders among the players. He was right, though it's ironic that a few years later the same bunch of players were accused by some people of running the team! He said the idea had come from Australian hockey. I have never had a problem with new or innovative ideas, as long as they work.

Colin Charvis, Martyn Williams, Robin McBryde and I were the quartet of co-captains. To be fair, Steve had made it clear Wales would only have one captain in the 2003 World Cup, but he wanted more people to take responsibility, on and off the field, for what was happening to the side. I think it worked, but you didn't see the benefit of the decision until much later on.

Being made Wales captain in 2006, when Gareth Jenkins was appointed coach, was the next time I would be given the job. It didn't faze me at all. I had captained most sides I had played for and had been the captain of a Wales Under-21 side that had won a Grand Slam. As fly-half, I was one of the leaders anyway and was one of the most vocal in the side.

There was a bit of furore about my appointment at the time, and talk that it was a real snub for Gareth Thomas. Alfie was his usual incredibly supportive self, but I didn't really view it as a great change for me. As the outside-half, I was always asked and had always given my opinion about what the team was doing anyway. Gareth Jenkins and I went back years and had a good relationship, and he wanted to work with somebody he knew. People forget that when Gareth was appointed Wales coach, the 2007 World Cup was just around the corner and that was the primary focus for everybody. Gareth had something like 18 months to put things in place for the tournament in France and, while most coaches have four years to build a squad, he knew he didn't have much time to make any mistakes. He had been given a two-year contract and knew France 2007 was when he would be judged.

The captain of any team is the bridge between the management, coaches and players, and Gareth wanted somebody who would tell him what he needed to know about the squad. I have never been a 'yes man' and have always thrown in my opinion about how and where any side I have been a part of needs to improve. The last thing you need is a 'nodding dog' environment because that can lead to frustration and misunderstanding. It's not healthy in any set-up, and coaches have to be secure enough to hear things they don't like, and players certainly have to be the same.

Being a captain is a hard job because you are managing so many different characters and players with different levels of experience. I have been lucky throughout my career – I cannot think of one captain who I didn't relate to or respect. It would have broken me if I'd had a captain who talked rubbish or who I wasn't able to work for, though I have noticed that the older I get, the harder I am to please. Now I have an opinion on what the team should be doing and am not afraid to voice that opinion. A good captain will always encourage that, and always needs a good group of senior players around him. When you have senior players around you who are good leaders, good role models and ambassadors, it makes your job so much easier. They will make valid contributions, take their fair share of responsibility and take the pressure off you as captain. The idea that a captain can be all-seeing and is the be-all and end-all of a side's success is nonsense. All the good sides, effectively, police themselves and have high standards on and off the pitch. I don't think people really appreciate how important that is for any side. Things like turning up on time and all wearing the same training kit may sound boring and mundane, but they set the tone and culture of a successful sports team.

Some captains are great talkers before a game, some are great at reading what is happening during a game, and others just lead by example on the field. I had played under some great Wales captains, such as Rob Howley, David Young, Scott Quinnell, Colin Charvis and Gareth Thomas, and they all did the job their own way. They didn't try to be anyone else, rather concentrating on being themselves, and that is what I tried to do. They trained and played hard and led by example but were very different characters off the pitch.

I have played for captains who get very emotional before a game and some who are the complete opposite and will say the odd word here and there to particular players. Simon Easterby, the

Scarlets captain, is quiet but leads by example on the field. I always enjoyed what Robin McBryde had to say when he was captain. He has a great way with words and is a good speaker in the team room or dressing-room. A lot of what he used to say would strike a nerve with me and really hit home. I would always look forward to hearing what he had to say before a game because his thoughts would often echo mine, or he would put what I was feeling into words really well. I have always had a huge amount of respect for anybody who can stand up in front of a group of players or people and deliver a message in a succinct way. It is a real talent.

Charv was probably the most mentally tough captain I ever played for. During his time as captain, he was voted as the third most unpopular person in Wales, behind Osama bin Laden and Saddam Hussein. He is probably the only person who could have dealt with something like that. The criticism that came his way was like water off a duck's back. He is a such a big character and an incredibly tough bloke. Alfie always led by example but was so relaxed in the week of a game he made you realise playing for Wales was something to enjoy. Paul O'Connell, who captained the Lions in 2009, is another who really impressed me. Paul had a major job bringing four countries and four different rugby cultures together in a short space of time, and he did a great job. He cut through all the traditional rivalry and got us to gel as a squad in a truly remarkable way.

The bottom line, though, is that if a player needs a captain to motivate him to play, he shouldn't be there. It's my view that it's a player's responsibility and duty to be self-motivated. I have never expected a captain to say a couple of magic words to get me in the right zone to do my job on the pitch.

People often ask me if I regret being Wales captain, or if it had a detrimental impact on my game. I would certainly do the job again, and at the time I didn't think it affected my performances, but our results while I was skipper certainly weren't great.

I took quite a bit of criticism as captain, with people claiming I shouldn't even have been in the side. It didn't really bother me because I have always felt everybody is entitled to his or her opinion, and I will always respect that. Everybody likes it when you are tapped on the back and you also have to cop it when people are having a go at you. It's part and parcel of professional sport today and you learn to detach yourself from the good and bad things that are said or written about you. It was my family and friends who suffered much more than me. They would hear something said on the TV or radio or during a game and get upset about it. Or they would read something in a newspaper and fail to understand why the criticism had to be so personal. Seeing them upset was hard to deal with, but my response was always pretty simple: don't watch it, don't listen to it and don't read it.

I have to admit I was pretty naive about what the role entailed. I knew there would be much more media work and that I was, effectively, the face of Welsh rugby, but I didn't really appreciate what that meant. I had seen Alfie do the job and he had carried on as normal, so I thought I could do the same. I thought being Wales captain was all about what you did on the pitch and what you did in the team environment. It isn't at all. You are public property and there to be shot at for any of the ills of the national side. The Wales captain is accountable, just like the Wales coach.

It's a high-profile role and your performances and your leadership of the team are a talking point in every pub, club, home, cornershop and cafe across the country. I thought it was just a rugby job, and that as long as you had the respect of the coaches and players that was enough. I was wrong about that, but the run of bad results while I had the job certainly didn't help.

Would I do things differently? With hindsight, of course I would. I think I focused a bit too much on being captain and I allowed myself to get caught up with some of the criticism that came my way.

Every player knows when he has played well or played badly, and I am no different. Looking back, I think I had slipped back into the same old routine when I returned to Wales. I had been home a year and while the Scarlets were firing on all cylinders and doing really well in Europe, I didn't challenge myself enough in the Test match arena. Players sometimes find it hard to see where they really are and that is why good coaches are so important: they will challenge you and tell you when you aren't playing well. The bottom line is that my performances weren't good enough. I know that now.

A young player called James Hook had also just catapulted himself into the limelight with some superb performances for the Ospreys and for Wales and he'd caught everybody's eye. Hooky, in fact, was the best thing that could have happened to me. Sometimes we take what we have for granted and he certainly brought out the best in me. I am a competitive animal and love the challenge of having to prove myself. That was something I certainly had to do when he arrived on the scene.

Hooky's emergence as a genuine rival for the number 10 jersey gave me the kick up the backside I needed. He is a fantastic rugby player, incredibly talented and has his feet on the ground. His natural ability is second to none and the competition between the pair of us pushed me on again. For the first time for a number of years, I knew that my name wouldn't automatically be read out on the team sheet. As a player, I need competition and Hooky kept me out of my comfort zone. His performances for Wales were superb. His composure and calmness, for someone so young, are miles ahead of anything I showed when I was his age. I was a much more excitable character then, but he seems to have ice in his veins and takes everything in his stride.

The 2007 Six Nations campaign was certainly one to forget, both for Wales as a country and from a personal point of view. We only won one game, against England, during the tournament and I was watching from the stands at the Millennium Stadium. Other than that the tournament is remembered for the controversy surrounding referee Chris White's decision to blow the final whistle early after we had kicked to touch in the dying moments, trying to salvage a victory from a very tough afternoon against Italy in Rome. Once again, I was off the field, having been battered and targeted by the Italians. I had four stitches in a cut above my left eye after being on the end of a knock by Italian flanker Mauro Bergamasco towards the end of the first half and had also suffered an injury to my hand. I went off for running repairs but started getting blurred vision in the eye and had to leave the field. It summed up my Six Nations and my season thus far. I was on a bad run and the harder I tried to put things right, the worse things got.

I did get a letter from Mauro a couple of days later, apologising for what he had done. I was impressed by the fact he had taken the time out to do that. Rugby does have a very unique culture and I am proud that it does. I cannot think of many other sports where an opponent would take the time to do something like that.

I didn't know how serious the hand injury was until training the following week. I went to catch a ball on the Monday in session and a shooting pain went straight up my arm. I was in agony. I went for a scan – we all thought it was just ligament damage, but I had actually fractured my thumb and I was out for a month. That meant I couldn't play against England in the final game and could only watch as the boys got an impressive 27–18 victory in Cardiff. It rescued a very disappointing Six Nations campaign for us.

Hooky had played really well and had gone through the score sheet, grabbing a try, a conversion, four penalties and a drop goal for his twenty-two points. I was captain, but I wasn't part of it, and it summed up my season at Test match level.

The next four weeks, recovering from the hand injury, were tough. When I finally did get back on the field, it was for the Scarlets in the Heineken Cup quarter-finals against Munster at Stradey Park. I had targeted that game as my return, and just running onto the field felt like a small victory, but a lot of my personal frustration came out in that game. People had been writing me off and I really felt I had a point to prove – to myself more than anybody else. Everything I did, I did with a real intensity and desire.

Ronan O'Gara, who is a great player and has been a great rival of mine down the years on the field, was up to all his old tricks on the pitch that night. Rog loves to trash-talk on the rugby pitch and really tries anything to get under your skin and put you off your stride. I had almost cuffed him after I had stamped on a Munster player's hand at a ruck to get the ball free. Rog took exception to what I had done. He didn't like my footwork and grabbed me, and we squared up to each other. I found myself screaming at him and nearly threw a punch. Luckily, I didn't. But the red mist had come down all around me. All the frustration of being criticised for being captain and my lay-off came to the surface in that one moment. I had him by the scruff of his neck and walked him back over to the corner flag, while Gavin Thomas scored a try in the other corner. I can remember shouting at him across the field, when we were both in our fly-half positions, and the Scarlets were ahead, 'Look at the scoreboard, Rog!'

We 'talked' to each other quite a bit that night at Stradey. I don't usually get involved with all of that stuff and try just to focus on the game, but I couldn't help myself. He had both barrels for most of that evening. I was an angry man and played with a really angry energy and purpose, which I think caught him completely unawares. It was one of those great European nights at Stradey Park. We were 17–0 ahead at half-time and would run out comfortable 24–15 winners. It would sum up that particular season. I would be in great form for the Scarlets, and thoroughly enjoyed my season with them, but my experience with Wales was the complete opposite. That, of course, would only add to the debate about being Wales captain, that my being captain was having an impact on performances in the international arena.

My agony with Wales would only get worse during the summer training camp we had organised out in France to acclimatise for the World Cup. I thought my run of bad luck was behind me and was determined to make the most of my third time at the tournament. I felt we had a really strong squad, with the perfect mix of experience and youth, and had a good draw. Nobody talked about it, but a semi-final place was a real possibility. I also had the added personal incentive of returning to the country where I had really enjoyed playing for Clermont. But at the training camp I tore a muscle in my groin and was in agony. I soon discovered it was a 50 per cent tear and I was in trouble.

I couldn't believe my luck. First, it was my thumb and now I had a problem with my groin. I wouldn't find out until much later, but if I had torn it any more I would have had to have the muscle reattached and would have been out of the World Cup, and probably out of action for a year, the longest I would ever have been out of the game. I was devastated. It was exactly the same injury endured by Rhys Williams, the Wales and Blues full-back, and he had been out of the game for ages.

I told Gareth Jenkins and he, quite rightly, started thinking about what he needed to do with the World Cup campaign just around the corner. He wanted some continuity and had a decision to make about who would captain Wales in the World Cup. He named Alfie on the eve of the tournament and, I have to say, I didn't have a problem with that. I was just delighted to be named in the World Cup squad and to have the opportunity to play for my country in the biggest rugby show on earth. Nobody really knew the full extent or the seriousness of my injury, but I owe so much to John Williams, the team doctor, and Mark Davies, the team physio, for getting me to France for the tournament. They did a fantastic job of taking care of me and getting me in some kind of condition to be declared fit for selection. I knew the seriousness of my injury after I had had a scan back in Wales and was told it could have got worse at any time during my rehab and recovery. I was just lucky I didn't need an operation.

Luckily, the human body showed what an amazing thing it is and the muscle just grew back. Even now I can remember the moment I thought my World Cup was over. I was at the Heath Hospital in Cardiff with John, the team doctor, having the scan. It was all going pretty normally when the specialist stopped and said,

'This isn't right.' When they told me what I had done, I was sure my World Cup was over.

I had been very lucky throughout my career in that I had never suffered a serious injury, but I knew this one had come at completely the wrong time. The World Cup was looming and it felt like I was in a race against time. The temptation to work harder to get back to fitness was at the forefront of my mind, but it was completely the wrong thing to do. I had to show some patience, something I don't have much of. Like every player, I have had my share of stitches, bumps and bruises, but nothing that has really kept me out of the game for too long. I have nothing but respect for players such as my Wales and Scarlets teammate Mark Jones, who spent two years out of action with two major knee injuries that could have ended his rugby career. Kevin Morgan, the Wales full-back, is another who has bounced back from so many major injuries. I hadn't experienced anything like the agony they had endured, so I know their mental toughness and resilience to keep going and finally play again deserves absolute respect. When you are injured, it is as if you are an outcast. You aren't part of the team and aren't part of the preparation for games, and it is a very lonely experience. Players and coaches do their best to keep you involved, but you just know you have nothing to offer. It is an incredibly frustrating time.

So, again, do I have regrets about being appointed Wales captain? No. Absolutely not. I don't even think it was a mistake taking the job because I was the Wales fly-half. I have heard the argument about the fly-half who runs the team on the field anyway not needing the extra responsibility of being captain, but that doesn't wash with me. Though I will admit the experience was another massive learning curve for me. I didn't really detach myself from being Wales captain and probably let it take over too much. Mind you, if I were asked to do the job again, I would accept it in a heartbeat.

In a funny way, the whole experience did re-energise me and ground me again. I rediscovered my love for the game and the values of hard work and doing the best I could for the team. My hunger to play well for my country burned deeper than ever and I feel the whole experience has stood me in good stead since. Everybody likes nice things being said about them, and nobody likes the bad things. I am no different. But nobody can be popular with everybody. Martyn Williams and I, who both had indifferent, shall we say, stints as Wales captain, always joke about the 'curse of the Welsh captaincy'. Dwayne Peel was probably the best at diffusing any tension or pressure I was feeling, with the odd well-placed remark. He had a way of putting the whole thing into perspective. If something went wrong in training, Peely would pipe up, 'Don't worry, Steve will cop it and get the blame anyway.' He brought a real gallows humour to my time as skipper.

It was a massive honour to captain my country. I will probably only realise and appreciate that I did the job when I have retired and have time to look back on my career.

CHAPTER 12

2008 GRAND SLAM

The trophy at the end is less important than the process itself.

– Roman Abramovich, Chelsea's billionaire owner

I **didn't expect to** make the World Cup in France because of injury, so when people ask me about the disappointment of that whole campaign it is tinged with the memory that I was fortunate to have been there. My groin injury was so serious that I really was up against it to get in the squad and only the great work of the medical team and the physios in the national set-up got me fit enough to play. Having said that, France 2007 was a major disappointment for everybody – the coaches, the players, the whole country. There is no getting away from that. I may not have been captain, after originally being appointed, but I didn't have any negative thoughts about losing that job. The reality was very simple: it was a World Cup, my third World Cup, and it was in France, a country I loved and in which I had enjoyed success with Clermont, and with Wales. Even now I find it hard to put my finger on what happened in that tournament – we just simply weren't at the races.

We had a great squad of players – a much stronger group of players than we had had four years earlier in Australia – but we didn't arrive in France with any great confidence or form and didn't really have any momentum behind us to speak of. In fact, we hadn't been playing well at all. We hadn't played well in the 2007 Six Nations, we had probably blown a victory over Australia in the first Test of the summer tour in Sydney and we had been pretty average in the World Cup warm-up games, although we did manage to beat Argentina in Cardiff. We had been humiliated by England in the World Cup warm-up game at Twickenham. We just hadn't got anywhere near playing to or realising the potential in the squad. We had plenty of talent but just didn't deliver. It was that simple and there are no excuses. I know people, especially in Wales, are always looking for somebody to blame, but that is the bottom line. There was no lack of effort or hard work: something was just missing.

Gareth Jenkins, my former Scarlets coach, was coach of Wales at the time and has taken the brunt of the blame for what happened in France, but the players have to take their share of responsibility for what happened, too. We were the ones on the field and we just didn't perform. People have suggested that the fact Gareth only had a two-year contract with the Welsh Rugby Union had a bearing on it, but it didn't affect the players.

I have to admit I was locked away in my own little bubble, away from the squad, for much of the build-up to the World Cup. I was fighting my own personal battle to get myself into some kind of condition just to be named in the team for the tournament. I had managed to get selected but had been out of action for three months before I came off the bench for the opening Pool game against Canada in Nantes.

Before the injury, thanks to great work by our fitness coach, Mark Bennett, I had been hitting personal bests in every aspect of my physical conditioning, but I hadn't done any real physical work since then and was nowhere near where I would have liked to have been physically, fitness-wise or rugby-wise. I hadn't played in any of the warm-up games or even trained in a match situation of any kind. Luckily, I hadn't lost any weight due to being on the physio table or in rehab, because my body weight is pretty constant and suits my frame.

I was happy to be on the bench, if a bit apprehensive, and we were 17–9 behind early in the second half when Gareth Thomas, Colin Charvis and I were called upon to bring us home. I had played my first 30 minutes of rugby and had come through it relatively unscathed. All three of us were credited with doing some kind of rescue job, but I always felt we would win the game because of our superior fitness. We all know Canada are a physical outfit, but I felt we were too strong for them. All I focused on was doing my job for the team and playing smart rugby.

We ran out comfortable 42–17 winners and had our first win of the tournament. I was relieved to have come through my first game of rugby for months. We then travelled home to play our next two games, against Japan and Australia at the Millennium Stadium in Cardiff. It was bizarre to be playing at home, when the World Cup was in France. We got a win over Japan, but lost 32–20 to Australia. We then returned to France to face Fiji in a game we had to win to qualify for the quarter-finals.

Everybody knows what happened next. We lost to Fiji in what everybody described as the best game of the tournament, but that certainly wasn't any consolation for us. Back in 2003, we had played in two of the best games of the tournament against New Zealand and England and were satisfied we had played to our potential. This time around it was the complete opposite, because we hadn't come close to achieving our potential. The 2007 World Cup was all about complete under-achievement by Wales. I know people expect me to blame this or that for the failure, but that is missing the point completely. We all failed in France in 2007. We didn't perform and hadn't done so long before we got there. We seemed to be on a downward spiral and couldn't get out of it.

I hit the post three times against the Fijians, something I will struggle to do again on a rugby field: it summed up where we were as a team. We lost 38–34, but I still cannot believe we leaked 30-odd points to the Fijians. The current Wales side would never do that. To be knocked out of the World Cup in France was humiliating for everyone, especially for a side which I still believe had so much to offer that tournament. We hadn't even reached the knockout stages and we were going home. Our World Cup was over.

We were so confident that we would beat Fiji and would be in Marseilles for the quarter-finals, the thought of being knocked out of the tournament in the Pool stages hadn't even crossed our minds. I was completely gutted by what had happened and had such a range of emotions going through my mind. It went from anger and frustration to disbelief, and back again. I was so wrapped up in trying to work out what had gone wrong that the ramifications for Gareth didn't really register with me.

It really hit home when he walked off the team bus at the entrance to the team hotel back in Cardiff and turned around and said, 'All the best, boys, and thanks. No regrets.' The number of cameras and journalists waiting for the team coach as we rolled into the hotel car park just underlined what had happened. The post-mortem had begun and the witch-hunt had started. Everybody was looking for a scapegoat and somebody to blame.

It was an emotional time for me. In 24 hours, we had been knocked out of the World Cup, let ourselves down, let our country down and lost our coach. Our plans to travel to Marseilles to play South Africa, the eventual world champions, in the quarter-finals were scrapped and we flew home. To say everybody was all over the shop would be an understatement. It was carnage. Sometimes as a player you can be so cocooned and locked into the process of trying to produce performances and win games that you don't really appreciate the ramifications of what is happening around you. It was only when I returned home to Wales and talked to my family, friends and people on the street that I really appreciated what had had happened. The media had gone into overdrive and the ritual post-mortem was particularly brutal for Gareth. He was blamed for everything, and I really felt for him because we were all responsible for what had happened. I know there was talk of the players wanting to play one way and the coaches another, but there hadn't been any clash as far as I could see. The approach we adopted was based on the 2005 Grand Slam style. Gareth wanted us to play and show off our skills but wanted us to have variety in our game; we all knew that we couldn't just throw the ball around and expect to win.

The bottom line is that we had been given everything by the Welsh Rugby Union and hadn't done ourselves justice or taken the opportunities we had been given. Gareth is a good bloke, a passionate rugby man, and he had waited so long to be Wales coach. What happened to him was very unpleasant. Nobody wanted Wales to be successful more than him, but he knew, win or lose, he was in the firing line. His fate after that World Cup illustrates the ruthless side of professional sport at the highest level. He understood that side of things just as well as anybody else, and so did all of the players, but it doesn't make what happened to him any easier to deal with. The pair of us had shared some great times together: France 2007 was the lowest point of my career with him as coach.

As a player, all sorts of things go through your head when you come home after being knocked out after a World Cup early. Will I be around for the next tournament? Is that my last experience playing in rugby's showpiece tournament? What a waste of all that hard work! We had the nucleus of the 2003 World Cup side in 2007, so where did it all go wrong? Even now, the tournament is hardly ever mentioned by any player who was there in France. We can discuss the 2003 World Cup in Australia until the cows come home, but not France 2007. All I know is that everything that could go wrong, did go wrong.

My opinion of the tournament as a whole will always be clouded by what happened to Wales, but for the genuine rugby supporter it must have been frustrating, because the teams that did well weren't the most exciting. South Africa, England, France and Argentina all reached the semi-finals, but they weren't the most exciting sides to watch, and all play a similar style of rugby. It was low-risk stuff, with big defences, physical packs and a kicking number 10. I watched the final between South Africa and England in Paris on TV and had nothing but admiration for the old enemy. They played to their potential and their strengths and knew what they were good at. Wales hadn't done that and we had just got lost somewhere.

After the World Cup, Phil Davies told me to take some time off and get away from rugby for a while, to give me a chance to get over my disappointment. I took Gwen to New York for four days and had a great break. Nobody knew who I was or what had happened in France or wanted to talk about rugby with me. We had a fantastic time and really chilled out. When I got home, I was ready to throw myself back into life with the Scarlets.

As I have become older, I have learnt to deal with the disappointments I have had in my career. That doesn't mean defeats get easier, but I can put them away now and move on. I was soon totally engrossed in the process of playing for the Scarlets, and what had happened with Wales was pushed to the back of my mind. I didn't dwell on France, but I knew we had butchered a great opportunity at the 2007 World Cup.

Warren Gatland, the former Ireland and London Wasps coach, succeeded Gareth as Wales coach. Like everybody else, I knew of his success with both of those sides but next to nothing about him as a man or a coach. I didn't know what his rugby philosophy was, what he wanted from his players, what type of players he liked or what style of rugby he wanted to employ. Warren would be my seventh Wales coach in nearly a decade of playing Test match rugby. All I knew was that everything would change and I would have to prove myself all over again.

When a new national coach comes in, every player wants to know his ideas about the game, but is also very aware that they have to find some form for their region or club. I knew Warren would turn up to watch the Scarlets and would run the rule over my performance, but also everybody else's in the side. When he arrived, I didn't have any real form and it wasn't a great time for me. I'd had a decent game against the Ospreys, but there wasn't much for him to get excited about what he'd seen since he'd arrived. In the previous season, the Scarlets had won six out of six in our Heineken Cup Pool matches and reached the semi-finals, but when he arrived we weren't performing at all. I hadn't shown any kind of form, so to speak, for him to be able to select me.

I was named in his Six Nations squad but wasn't selected in the starting line-up for the opener against England at Twickenham. I was hugely disappointed, but I couldn't argue with his selection because I hadn't shown him anything on the pitch. It was time to dig in and let him know I could buy into the whole squad ethos and put the work in on the training pitch. Warren took some stick for picking 13 Ospreys for the trip to face the World Cup finalists, but I thought it was a very smart move by him. He hadn't been in the country very long and hadn't really had any time to work with the squad, and he made it easy for the players and the coaches to get down to work. He told us he would select players on what he saw, not by reputation or what somebody had told him or what we had achieved before. The slate was, effectively, wiped clean.

He had explained to me where I was in his thoughts. He said he knew I had been a regular for Wales and promised me I would get an opportunity to show what I could do on the pitch during the tournament. He was true to his word and that is all any player wants. He made it very clear I was behind James Hook in the pecking order for the number 10 shirt and I really couldn't argue with his reasons for that. He told me I had work to do – he was very straight with me, told me what was expected from me and what my role was in the team. He was a straight-talker; everything was black and white. I knew I had a point to prove.

Almost as soon as Warren arrived, things changed overnight. He made the process of training and playing paramount in everybody's thoughts. He brought a new structure to nearly everything and with it a really steely edge to what we were doing. We had a different focus and mindset almost immediately when we turned up for the first session. All of us were told, in no uncertain terms, what our responsibilities were and what would be totally unacceptable. There was no place to hide and reputations counted for nothing. He would only deal with what he saw in our performances.

Warren brought in Shaun Edwards, the Wasps head coach and rugby league legend, and Rob Howley, the former Wales captain, and they quickly established a new routine, with high standards, and created a ridiculously competitive environment. They challenged us at every turn and it was made very clear that being the best in the UK or Britain wasn't enough, they wanted Wales to be the best in the world. Everything was different, from the training on the field to the weights sessions, even down to how every player's performance in a game was broken down and measured. The rugby sessions were short, sharp and very intense and done at a game-like intensity. Training wasn't niggly, but every one of us knew our skills were being scrutinised and analysed like never before.

All of the players could feel the impact of what we were doing almost straight away. We were stronger, dealt with the contact area in a much more aggressive way and were getting back into position for the next phase or moving much more quickly than we had before. I had been around the national set-up for a while, but everything they did to challenge the players was incredibly stimulating. It was the attention to detail of the whole process that stunned me. The coaches weren't just looking at your performance in training but how you were throughout the whole week. Were you buying into what they were doing? Were you being open and honest about what you were doing? They looked at the whole package and everything was designed to have an impact on what we did during a game. They also had no qualms about telling you when you did something wrong, but, more importantly, they told you why it was wrong and what you had to do to put it right.

The impact on a group of players who had been knocked out of the World Cup only a few months earlier was unbelievable. In particular, Warren reminded us of what an honour it was to play for Wales and that we should never take it for granted. He talked about Wales being a proud rugby nation and said that we should all respect that.

He saw real potential in all the players he had selected. He had picked a small squad and made it clear that everybody would play in the Six Nations and those not initially selected had to train hard and be patient. It meant we all knew we would not be holding tackle bags for a couple of months or be cannon fodder for 22 players selected for the first match. He also rammed home the fact that we had to make the most of every opportunity we were given. We would be a team renowned for its hard work and would be expected to work hard for each other and the red jersey. They pushed us out of our comfort zone. We all wanted to do our best for them and hit the standards they had introduced. Our approach to the game did change, which was expected when you look at the stature and size of the players in the squad, and we played to those strengths.

Being on the bench for the England game was a new experience for me – it was the first time I hadn't started a Six Nations game, when fit, for a long, long time. It was sobering and rammed home to me where I was in the pecking order, and also the challenge that lay in front of me. As I watched the first half, I saw us hang on for long periods, but we stuck to the game plan devised to beat England. At half time, the message was clear and to the point: stick to the game plan and the rewards will come, and that is exactly what happened in the last 20 minutes of the game. The coaches had got it spot on and we had beaten England at Twickenham for the first time since 1988. Wales, a team that hadn't even got out of their World Cup Pool, had beaten the World Cup finalists in their own backyard. It was a new dawn and the team's confidence just soared. We were on a roll again.

I came off the bench for the Scotland game and played for 30 minutes. All I can remember thinking was, don't play like a monkey, and make the most of your opportunity. All I could think was: stick to the game plan, do your role for the team and don't do anything flashy. It wasn't an audition, but a chance to show I had listened and taken on board what the coaches had been talking about and was good enough to be in the squad and to wear the jersey. We had a good win against the Scots in Cardiff and my reward was to be selected with Dwayne Peel at half-back for Italy's visit. Italy are always a physical test for any side, but we had worked hard on our fitness and played a high-tempo game. We worked very hard, knowing they would crack in the second half. That's exactly what happened, and that was when the strength of the current Wales squad was rammed home to me. Peely and I, two Lions, were now battling with two future Lions, Hooky and Mike Phillips. Nobody was safe when it came to selection because the competition for places was so intense.

Our next game was against the Irish in Dublin and was billed as the great grudge match between Warren and Eddie O'Sullivan, his successor as Ireland coach. There was supposed to have been some animosity between them because of the way Warren lost his job with Ireland, but he never mentioned it to the Welsh players. He didn't seem uptight or anything like that and was pretty relaxed about all the stuff being played out in the press. One of Warren's great strengths is that he is very constant as a coach and doesn't go through great emotional peaks and troughs. He makes it very clear he is here to win and that is what our jobs are. All of the players knew Ireland away was the big one; we didn't have a great record there and were playing for a Triple Crown.

I was in the starting line-up, and we performed really well and showed some real mental toughness when we lost Mike Phillips and Martyn Williams to yellow cards. We had bought into Warren's philosophy and it was a very different Wales performance from that expected from us. We had matured as a team, knew the options we could call on and played streetwise rugby to the letter of the law. I missed my first kick at goal but got my next three, but our victory will always be remembered for Shane Williams' try in the corner. He was on fire. I don't think many other players could have scored a try like that in such little space. It was breathtaking. Gavin Henson also had one of his best games in a Wales shirt and summed up the new approach we had adopted. He was our defensive captain and did his homework on all the teams; he was a great leader of our defensive patterns. He was also very vocal, and people don't see that side of him in a game. Gav loves his big hits and put in a massive hit on Shane Horgan, which gave us all a massive lift. He also produced a huge relieving kick at a critical point in the game. All in all, everybody was doing their bit and more for the team, and we came away with a 16–12 victory and the Triple Crown. We were buzzing and all knew a second Grand Slam was now a real possibility.

Being in the bubble of the Wales squad and locked into the process of training, playing and winning means talk of Grand Slams or wooden spoons doesn't really seep into your consciousness. You are on the match-by-match roller coaster and enjoying the moment, or trying to put things right, but we were all made very aware what was at stake against France at the Millennium Stadium: a Grand Slam.

I hadn't made the best start against Ireland, especially in the first 15 minutes, and I knew I was on a knife edge when it came to being selected to play against the French. If I am honest, I knew what was coming, but still hoped I would get the nod. I was kicking with Tom Shanklin in the WRU's training barn at the Vale of Glamorgan when I caught sight of Warren walking over to me. For me, it was the longest walk Warren has ever taken, and he probably doesn't even realise that, but when he finally asked if he could have a quick word with me I knew I hadn't made the starting line-up.

'Steve,' he said. 'I am not going to select you for France.' He told me he had decided to go with Hooky, but that I would get a run at some point in the game. He turned around and walked away and I was devastated. Not getting selected is the hardest part of being a sportsman, though I appreciated that he had told me face-to-face before the team was announced. If I ever learn to accept non-selection, I know it's time for me to walk away from the game. Warren had taken the time to tell me I wasn't in the side, and he didn't have to do that.

I did come off the bench when the score was 9–9, and we ran out 29–12 winners and, of course, won the Grand Slam. Winning the 2008 Grand Slam was fantastic, but what was more enjoyable was the whole process of getting there. I found it very satisfying, though it still didn't ease the frustration of our failure at the World Cup only five months earlier. In fact, it made it even more disappointing. The same core group of players who had failed in France were now European champions. We had played to our potential and shown what we were capable of. In some ways, it was a relief that we had proved we were a good side. It meant all the talk that we were flash in the pan, not fit enough, didn't play a high enough standard of rugby, and that the Magners League was not intense enough, was a total nonsense. We had trained in a different way, done our homework and learnt from the experience of France 2007. We had shown we could adapt to a different style of play and hit our potential. What that whole season proved to me was that rugby, or any sport, is just a roller coaster.

It was the strangest season of my whole career. I had to deal with the disappointment of the World Cup at the start of it and had won a Grand Slam by the end of it. I had gone from being captain to not being selected in the starting line-up . . . but it would get even more bizarre on our summer tour to South Africa.

I often get asked about the impact Warren and Shaun, in particular, have had on Wales and what they are like as people. Warren has assembled a fantastic team around him, with Rob, Craig White, our fitness guru, and the analysis team. He is a great speaker, very clever and has a great feel for where his players are, physically and mentally. There is no doubt he has raised the bar in the squad and expects – and demands – high standards. He wants Wales to be a success and he sees no reason why we shouldn't be. His whole manner and approach inspire self-belief and confidence in players. He has told us what we need to be a success and that we will be breaking new boundaries with Wales. We may have had success in the '50s and the '70s, but he wants us to achieve a sustained period of success. He has taken us into new territory and even the young players are made aware of the responsibility of playing for Wales. He is the boss and wants to take us to another level.

Shaun is a unique character. He is a fantastic defence coach and has even managed to persuade Welsh players, who love to play with the ball rather than tackle, that defence can be enjoyable and a statement about ourselves as players and as a team. Everybody thinks all he does is rant and rave, but he is very approachable and his technical and tactical knowledge is second to none. He knows the detail of the game and wants to improve players, but he also isn't afraid to tell you what he thinks, or to challenge his players. He hammers home what he expects from his players and demands everything. He played at the highest level in rugby league and instinctively understands what players want and need from a coach. He can break down the opposition and knows the strengths and weaknesses of his own players. He knows what feet players like to step off on and when a player is getting ready to carry a ball. Shaun is also very passionate about his players and his team, but more importantly the game as a whole: he just loves rugby. He enjoys success, but does take defeat very personally.

Warren, Shaun and Rob all hit you with facts about your game and believe hard work will bring its own rewards. Their after-match debriefs can be pretty brutal – they will ask you why you did this or that in the game. Or, why you didn't do this or that when you had the ball. They want players to take responsibility and all they ask is that you give it everything when you run out onto the field. If you do so and still lose, they will accept that. If you don't and lose, they let you know it's unacceptable. All three of them are rugby fanatics and if you have lunch with them, they are always talking about the game, the latest innovation or a new player they have watched. They are always discussing and throwing new ideas out to be chewed over and are constantly looking to improve. I know the public see Shaun, in particular, as being pretty intimidating, but that couldn't be further from the truth. His door is always open and he will listen to what you have to say and discuss everything and anything. All three of them are the same: they are all very approachable and always bounce new ideas off you. Another thing they share is that they are excellent at their jobs.

The next challenge was the summer tour and would be our first experience of seeing Warren and Shaun when they had lost a game. Up until then, we had only experienced what it was like to be part of a winning dressing-room with them in charge. Wales, the European champions, flew out that summer to face South Africa, the world champions, in their own backyard. I got the nod at fly-half and we started well but fell away pretty badly and were on the end of a 43–17 beating in the first Test in Bloemfontein. We had been beaten badly and it was a real kick up the backside for everybody. We had gone on tour believing we could beat the Boks. Warren made no secret of how unhappy he was in the dressing-room after the defeat. He told us he felt humiliated and shared that with the public and we were left under no illusions how bad he felt about that defeat. He was brutally honest with every player but he didn't throw empty statements about. He told us we hadn't come close to playing well, but all the players knew that anyway. He told us a performance like that might have been acceptable in the past but it was not acceptable while he was in charge. I would like to think he got the response he wanted from us because nobody had a beer after that game and everybody was up early on their laptops the following morning, poring over footage of the game and analysing where we had gone wrong. We all knew we had a chance to put it right at the end of the week in the second Test in Pretoria. It was also a sign of the new culture and, I would like to think, the character in the squad. It was all about starting the process and fixing what we had done wrong and getting the job done. We hadn't done ourselves justice and we wanted to do that in the second Test. Before we could do that we had to share a plane with the Boks on the Sunday, and that certainly added to our motivation. We didn't beat the world champions in the second Test but we came bloody close. They were rocking midway through the second half when we should have been awarded a penalty try when Alun Wyn Jones was robbed of the ball on their line. The game turned on that moment and our chances of a first win on South African soil went with it. We had pushed the world champions to breaking point, thanks to the smallest player on the pitch, a certain Shane Williams. Shane was brilliant in the game and had a real Roy of the Rovers game. He seemed able to beat players at will and his footwork, on the hard grounds, was extraordinary. As the fly-half, when you have a player like that in your side, you just give him the ball as often as he wants it. You follow him and support him but really you just watch him go and let him express himself. It was no surprise he was voted the International Rugby Board World Player of the Year in 2008 after the season he'd had. But the game in Pretoria was when I had my strangest experience ever on a rugby field as a player. I lined up two kicks at goal during that game and each time a little green lazer-like light flickered across the sweet spot of the ball. It was obviously deliberate and designed to put me off my stride and my kicking routine and to make me miss the kick. I am not suggesting it was a ploy any of the Springboks were aware of, but somebody in the crowd knew what they were doing and tried to stop me from kicking those points. They were only half successful; I missed one of them and slotted the other over.

The South Africa tour confirmed to me what a good state Welsh rugby is now in. Back in 1998, I had won my first cap for Wales against the then world champions, the Springboks, in South Africa and had been on the end of a 90-point hiding. I know a whole batch of first-team players were missing, but ten years on we were one controversial incident from beating the world champions in their own backyard. We are now a good side, with very ambitious players and coaches, and should take confidence from that. We had also shown we had some character in the squad in the way we had knuckled down and bounced back after the first Test. Some Welsh teams would have already been thinking of the off-season after a defeat like that, but we wanted to prove we were still a good side. The coaches also knew what we were made of. We lost the second Test 37–21 and the series 2–0, but we had risen to the challenge and proved we were a good side.

The autumn of 2008 will be remembered for one incident more than any other, even our victory over Australia that November. That was Wales's decision not to retreat after the All Blacks had done their traditional haka ahead of the game at the Millennium Stadium. The New Zealand boys didn't really know what to do when they saw we hadn't moved from our line after they had issued their traditional challenge to us. Apart from actually playing in games, it has to be my most memorable moment on a rugby field. It was a brilliant experience and such a buzz to be stood there with your teammates against the best rugby nation on the planet. I love the haka and my abiding memory of facing it in Wales is always the camera flashes going off all the way through it and the noise of the Welsh crowd as they try to drown the All Blacks' chants out. This time, though, was extra special. We knew we were going to do something and Warren, the coaches and management, had a range of options to choose from. Warren, as a former All Black, would have known more about it than anyone else and that New Zealand would have expected us to turn away first. The players bought into it straight away and really wanted to do what had been suggested and that's what we did. I can remember Jonathan Kaplan, the South African referee, telling Ryan Jones, our captain, after we had been there about a minute, with the crowd noise getting louder and louder, to move. Ryan just kept replying: 'Tell them to move.' Brilliant. I loved that whole experience and it was a bit different from what Sir Clive Woodward's Lions came up with for the tour to New Zealand in 2005. Brian O'Driscoll, our Lions captain, picked up a blade of grass and threw it in the air after the haka in the first Test, with Peely, as the youngest player and our youngest warrior, alongside him. I always had problems with Peely as a warrior and I still rib him about that now! But after the massive adrenaline rush of our stand-off to the haka in 2008, it was down to yours truly to kick the match off. The last thing I wanted after that great moment of sporting theatre was to kick the ball straight out into touch, but I was so pumped up that I had to take some time out to compose myself for the job in front of us. Kicking the ball out on the full, or not kicking the ball ten metres, would have been a real damp squib for everyone.

That autumn campaign was all about going to the next level. Warren had drilled into us that it was time to take the next step and to get a big scalp of one of the southern hemisphere sides. We were lined up to play South Africa, New Zealand and Australia in Cardiff but we produced a mixed bag throughout that campaign. We blew our chance against South Africa with a poor start, started well against New Zealand but fell away in the second half. We hadn't put an 80-minute performance together until we beat Australia. We were the better team on the day and played for the whole game, showing we were still heading in the right direction and that we had improved. We had eradicated the errors in our game and learned from our mistakes. We already knew we were capable of beating England and France, but now we had shown we could beat one of the 'big three'.

Before the win over the Wallabies, Warren had used me as a guinea pig to the other players during a training session to highlight the ability to think and react when under pressure in key moments in a game. We were in the middle of a typically intense session when he decided I had to kick a penalty with the whole squad gathered around me. I put my kicking tee down and started to go through my usual routine, when all the banter started from the players: 'This is why you get paid the big money,' somebody said, and then it all started. Even my run-up was scrutinised and I had to put up with the 'whoa' that goalkeepers in football have to put up with from the crowd when they kick. It certainly wasn't Thomond Park, but I managed to convert the kick and Neil Jenkins was behind the posts going berserk and screaming like any Welsh fan. I managed to kick OK against the Wallabies, but did miss a couple.

The win over the Wallabies was a vindication of what we had been doing and proved we were on the right track. Warren makes a big point about channelling our emotion and feeding off the crowd but remembering to stick to the process, the game plan and what we want to do in a game. I can remember times when emotion was the only thing I certainly played off and when I would get too caught up in my desire to do well. If you get too emotional before or during a game, you end up playing like headless chickens and inevitably lose. In 2002 or 2003 we certainly played like that, because we didn't really know any other way. We were working hard but didn't know how to play intelligent rugby.

Wales entered the 2009 Six Nations campaign as the favourites and the team to beat, but the main goal for us was to back up the Grand Slam in 2008 with good performances and to play to a consistently high level. I think we achieved that, even though we finished fourth in the tournament. We played really well against Scotland, we beat England again for the third consecutive time in the Six Nations, although I did get a text from Tony Marsh in France for tackling one of the English boys after he had scored a try. It read: 'There is no point tackling a player after he has scored a try!' We produced a great performance in Paris against France but lost because we made costly mistakes at critical times in the game. The reaction of the French players at the end of the game once they had won proved how far we had come as a team. It wasn't great to get beaten, but it showed the respect they had for us, and their conservative approach to the game was also a real compliment to us. It all proved that Wales are now a different proposition and a scalp for the teams we play against.

The last game of the Six Nations was against Ireland, who were going for a first Grand Slam since 1948. A Welsh victory would have secured a Triple Crown, and we had to win by 13 points to win the Six Nations title. It was a great game and a really enjoyable one to play in, despite the result. It was a real Test match between two very good sides and was one of the most intense and physical I have played in. Wales and Ireland have developed a really healthy rivalry over the last few years but Ireland have had the upper hand for most of that time. The Irish provinces of Munster and Leinster have won the European Cup three times, while Wales is still waiting to see if a Welsh region can do the same. But the gap between the sides has closed in recent years and I can only see any Welsh–Irish contest getting bigger and better in the future. The game had it all and literally went down to the last kick, or last missed kick. Both sides knew we had enough to play for with all the trophies at stake, but on top of that was the fact that this game was being billed as an unofficial trial for the Lions tour to South Africa at the end of the season. I know there was a lot of talk about Ronan O'Gara and Stephen Jones's personal battle for the Lions number 10 spot against the Springboks. So there was everything to play for, and so much at stake for, players in both sides. Rog, to his credit, delivered when it mattered, he had two moments in the game to make a difference for his team and he did it. His cross-kick for Tommy Bowe's try and his drop goal with three minutes to go clinched the victory. I had dropped a goal with five minutes to go to put us in the lead but knew Ireland still had plenty of time to score again. I then sliced a kick after the re-start and put the ball out on the full, when Mike Phillips was going to kick the ball long. There was a breakdown in communication somewhere and the ball came to me and I didn't deal with it very well. I then had a chance to win the game with a long-range penalty with the last kick of the game and it fell just short. We had lost 17–15 and I was inconsolable and lost in my own little world, replaying what had just happened in my head, and walking off the field to the sanctuary of the dressing-room. It was only then that I felt a tap on my shoulder and it was Rog, who had run all the way from beneath the Irish posts, and he said: 'Great game. Well played and see you in South Africa.' It was a nice touch and I appreciated what he'd just done, and we swapped jerseys on the field. We have had some great personal battles down the years but we have always got on well. His kind words didn't ease my pain and I knew I had had an opportunity to win the game and hadn't taken it. After the defeat, much was said about all the hype and mind games before the game and whether Warren had wound the Irish boys up by some of the things he said. All I know is that all of that stuff doesn't really affect players or a team. It's brilliant for the public, but if a player cannot get motivated to play for his country, he shouldn't be playing the game. I have never struggled for motivation and my competitive streak always kicks in before and during a game. If somebody has given me a clip during a previous meeting, I do remember it but you cannot go over the top about those things because it can cloud your judgement and obscure what your role for the team is.

I often get asked which was the better achievement, the Grand Slam in 2005 or the Grand Slam in 2008? It's an almost impossible question to answer. The first Grand Slam did look like it was going to be a flash in the pan after the disappointments in the 2006 Six Nations, but people forget the amount of injuries, due to the Lions tour of New Zealand, we had to contend with. I can remember Dick Best, the former England and Lions coach, claiming our success back then was built on sand. I didn't agree with him at the time but I can see what he meant now. Back in 2005 we had tasted our first real success and all believed what we were doing was right and that we had struck upon a winning formula. What we didn't have in 2005, which we had in 2008, was any real strength-in-depth. We probably had 20 international players and nowhere near the competition for places that we have now. I also realise now that there is more than one way to win a rugby game and we were a much better balanced and more mature side, who could adapt to different situations, in 2008. I also think that the current Wales set-up will deliver consistently high performances over the next few seasons. But what both sides shared was a commitment to the process of playing, ahead of winning, and that process ended with them both winning a Grand Slam.

CHAPTER 13

THE LIONS

The easy bit has passed. Selection for the Test team is the easy bit. This is your fucking Everest, boys . . . To win for the Lions in a Test match is the ultimate. They don't rate you. They don't respect you. The only way to be rated is to stick one on them.

– Jim Telfer, assistant coach of the Lions in South Africa in 1997

Playing for the British and Irish Lions is the pinnacle. Playing for Wales and representing my country is everything, but the Lions is different. It is special because it only happens every four years, but the magic of a Lions tour is that the team will never play together again after that particular tour. Everybody has grown up with and is aware of the great history and tradition of what is the last great rugby tour. I was lucky enough to be selected for two Lions tours, to New Zealand in 2005 and South Africa in 2009. I enjoyed both, though they were very different.

What always astounds me is the media coverage and debate a Lions tour generates. It is like a beast that just comes alive and then goes back to sleep for four years. There really is nothing quite like it. It really captures everybody's imagination, not just that of the rugby fans.

In 2005, I was playing in France and knew the Lions tour was on the horizon, but in Clermont I was pretty much sheltered from all the hype. It was only when I returned to Wales, or talked to family and friends, that I got a real feeling for all the talk of the tour to New Zealand. In 2009, I was in Wales and everywhere you turned it was the Lions being discussed. People would ask about the Lions selection and I would go through the ritual of telling people I wasn't thinking about it, just concentrating on playing well for Wales and the Scarlets. In reality, the Lions selection was always there in the background, nagging away at me. Have I done enough? Will that poor performance cost me a place? Will the coaches have noticed that mistake? I tried not to get too caught up in everybody's favourite pub game: what is your Lions Test side? It's just like that other favourite debating point: who should be Wales captain? And while the supporters of British and Irish rugby are marking out names, so are the players in their respective dressing-rooms. I have always tried to stay away from all of that because it is something I cannot control. I have always found it amazing that a player could have one good game and he, all of a sudden, gets to be a 2009 Lion. What I have learnt about the Lions selection is that there are very different criteria for players' selections. First, you will only be selected on form through a season, what role you can play in the squad and ultimately in the Test side. Second, a player's character and whether he is a good tourist are important, and then other players will be selected because they offer something different.

I knew I had a pretty good chance of making the trip, but I didn't take anything for granted. My form was good, and I was satisfied with my own performances for Wales during the Six Nations campaign and the job I had done for the team. We may not have won another Grand Slam, which was always going to be tough after winning it in 2008, but we still had a chance of winning the Six Nations in the final game against Ireland at the Millennium Stadium. I was being talked about as the Test number

10 and that was nice to hear, but I didn't get carried away with all of that stuff. I just knew I had to keep playing well.

Like every other player, I only found out I was selected after the squad was announced live on Sky Sports, and it was a relief more than anything. I watched it in the Scarlets team room, where there was a cheer and a round of applause when my name was read out. Matthew Rees, my fellow Scarlet, had what must have seemed like for ever to wait to find out if he had made it. His name was the last one read out. Smiler lived up to his nickname and had a broad grin on his face when it finally came.

It was a huge honour just to be named, but the Lions ask questions of players at every turn. You want to be named in the squad, then play well enough to make the Test side, and then win a Test series. A Lions Test series is so unique because it is the toughest environment for any rugby player. You are talking about effectively playing three World Cup finals on three successive Saturdays. It is physically and mentally draining, and like nothing else a rugby player will experience.

I was lucky to have that experience in my memory bank after the 2005 tour of New Zealand. Sir Clive Woodward, England's World Cup-winning coach, who took charge of the 2005 Lions, was slaughtered for the 3–0 Test series defeat to the All Blacks, but I didn't think he did much wrong at the time. He was criticised for taking too many staff, players and, of course, Alastair Campbell, Tony Blair's spin doctor, but I have always felt we just weren't good enough to win that series. I actually got on very well with Alastair, he was a fascinating bloke to talk to, and a good man.

With the luxury of hindsight, I think it's fair to say that Clive got some things wrong on the tour, but he gave the players everything they could have asked for. The attention to detail was staggering. I understood why England had won the World Cup in 2003! He tried to do what he had done with England, which made sense, because it had been a success for him, but the Lions are so very different from any other team.

In New Zealand, I started two of the three Test matches and came off the bench for my third Lions Test cap. Wearing the number 10 shirt for the first Test in Christchurch was a huge honour and my selection ahead of Jonny Wilkinson, who was selected at inside-centre, was a big talking point at the time. The only thing I can really say about that combination is that it didn't really work. I have been asked if I felt intimidated by having a World Cup-winning number 10 outside me, but that didn't even cross my mind. It was nobody's fault, but I don't think we got the best out of each other. I would like to think things would be different if we played alongside each other now, but back then we just had very different approaches to the game. I had just won a Grand Slam with Wales and wanted to attack and play from anywhere, while Jonny had won a World Cup with England by playing mistake-free rugby and to the strengths of a great pack. I don't think we were set in our ways, we just had different approaches. There is no wrong or right way, it was just a disappointment that we didn't click on the pitch. Mind you, I don't think it really mattered because we were playing one of the great All Black sides. The 2005 Lions just happened to come up against a Kiwi side that was at its peak and had swept away all before them.

The 2009 Lions tour was very different. We were playing the world champions in their own backyard, and it doesn't get bigger than that. The hype surrounding the tour had gone up another notch again, something I had thought was impossible. Ian McGeechan, who was on his umpteenth Lions tour as player and coach, made a point of trying to reclaim the Lions ethos and values, and that really struck a chord with all of us. The way the tour was structured and the attention to detail were just startling. The training week was intense but not too heavy, and nothing was left to chance, with the focus on peaking for every game and eventually the Tests against the Boks. Geech, Warren Gatland, Shaun Edwards, Rob Howley and Graham Rowntree all knew they had to manage players who had come off the back of a long season, and they did it really well.

I felt it was the little things, like all the players sharing rooms, something that we didn't do in New Zealand, which had such a big impact on the squad. It brought the squad together and it is funny how something like that can bring such a positive feeling to a Lions tour. I didn't really appreciate how important that kind of detail could be. It was these kinds of things that made the 2009 Lions tour one of the most enjoyable experiences of my career. I got to know people I had only ever lined up against on a rugby field. I knew what they were like as players, but I also got to know them as people, and there was not one bad apple in the squad. That, I can tell you, is very rare when you have a group of 35 professional players, let alone international players, in an intense environment like a Lions tour. You have 35 big egos, players who are first choices for their countries and are used to things being done in a particular way.

I found Geech to be a very impressive rugby man and a great bloke. We all knew that as head coach he was the man who would have the final say on selection. I had never really worked with him before and it was the first time he would get to see what I could do. I couldn't fault him and he didn't get carried away with anything; as far as I could see, he managed the ups and downs of the tour impressively. I shouldn't have been surprised by that because he is 'Mr Lions', and has a great rugby CV. You only have to look at what he has done as a player and a coach to see that. He was very approachable, very clear and precise, and his door was always open to anyone.

He had already done the 'easy part' by selecting a good group of people, as well as players, and he was very clever in managing the group dynamics of such a big squad. He made sure it wasn't a one-man show and brought everybody together, making us all feel part of the conspiracy, if you like. It cannot be underestimated how important that was. There was a fantastic team spirit and camaraderie within the squad. Geech just seemed to know instinctively what he was doing.

In 2005, we had two buses and the players were split between them. In 2009, we had two buses, but one was for all the players and the other for all the coaches and back-up staff. The players were never split up, and we became a unit because of that. We were given every chance to be successful, and even training for the third Test was managed superbly. We had a beaten and battered squad, and didn't train until the Wednesday before the game; the natural tendency of most coaches is to work their players hard after a defeat, but that didn't happen in South Africa. We were well looked after and had great coaches and staff on the tour, who knew when to ease off and allow the squad to rest. No stone had been left unturned and all the players appreciated it and flourished in the environment that had been created for us.

I shared a room with Paul O'Connell, the Lions captain. He had only ever been a pain in the arse to me when I had played against him, because he was always such an influential figure for Munster and Ireland. Paul is a great bloke and an inspirational skipper, and was a great leader of the 2009 Lions. He is a magnificent speaker and drew all of us together as soon as we met up for the week before we left for South Africa. His speeches about the responsibility we had for the Lions jersey, each other and ourselves were truly inspirational. He spoke about what the Lions meant to him and what a responsibility it was to be a Lions captain. He told us that he wished we could all be standing where he was, looking around the room and seeing the talent before him, and that it was a privilege to be leading us in South Africa. He said he saw a squad full of World Cup winners, Grand Slam winners, Heineken Cup winners and a World Player of the Year, and that he wouldn't want to be anywhere else or with anybody else than the 2009 Lions. He underlined the size of the task ahead of us and told us that we were in a mission-impossible situation; we would all be out of our comfort zones on tour, he said, but he wanted us all to embrace the moment and each other and the opportunity we had been given, and to have no regrets when the tour was finally over. He was a class act as a captain.

I am sure he won't mind me revealing what a sad pair of roommates we were. Once, we were both in our hotel room, sitting at our laptops, having a deep and detailed discussion. We stopped, then picked up on the same discussion moments later. We looked at each other when we realised what our conversation had been all about. We weren't talking about what a great country South Africa was or the whole Lions experience, or even what we had planned when the tour was over. The pair of us had been consumed talking about the intricacies and dynamics of back-row play! How sad is that? Even in our own time, away from team meetings or the team room, the pair of us were still talking about rugby!

Ronan O'Gara was another great rival I got to know really well on tour. We were both competing to be the Lions number 10 in the Test series and have had some great battles over the years at various levels of the game, but we spent a lot of time together in South Africa. Rog is rugby-intelligent and an incredibly mentally tough character. He has seen great highs and devastating lows with Ireland and Munster throughout his career, but has never buckled under the pressure or demands of being such a high-profile figure. He lives and moves in some incredible circles in Irish life but hasn't let it all go to his head. We had some great technical discussions about the game and kept pushing each other, but also supporting each other throughout the tour.

Some real characters did emerge on the tour and usually had us in stitches. Ugo Monye, the England and Harlequins wing, was our travel guide and took it upon himself to always give us a speech, detailing the history and facts and figures of every new place we had arrived in. Euan Murray, the Scotland prop, who is a born-again Christian, and Luke Fitzgerald, the Ireland wing, were designated as the 'Joke of the Day' team. They both had to deliver a joke, but it was Euan's deadpan delivery of some dreadful gags that would have us all in pieces. You had to be there to really to appreciate what I am talking about! He even left us a DVD he had filmed of himself telling jokes after he had left the tour early due to injury, which was always screened on the TV on the front of the bus. He was one of the good guys. Of the Welsh boys, Andy Powell was priceless. His duel with Donncha O'Callaghan, the Irish lock, for the microphone at the front of the bus was one of the most keenly contested battles of the tour.

Powelly was a real star of the tour and I had first-hand experience of that. We were both asked to film a good-luck message on behalf of the Lions for the British troops on the frontline in different parts of the world. I went first and said, 'To all the troops, best wishes and stay safe, on behalf of the 2009 Lions.' Powelly was next up and delivered the immortal line, 'Keep well and keep fighting.' I looked at him, not believing what I had just heard, and dissolved on the spot. Classic.

We opened the tour with a narrow 37–25 victory over a Royal XV in Rustenburg. It wasn't a great performance, but we got the win and the tour was on the road. I was due to make my first start of the tour in the second game of the tour against the Golden Lions at Ellis Park, Johannesburg. There was plenty of emotion swirling around inside, but I tried to keep a clear head and just focus on doing myself justice and running through the moves we were going to use. I couldn't have made a worse start if I'd tried. With my first touch of the ball, I spooned it and knocked it on from the kick-off. What a great way to start a Lions tour and lay a marker down for a Test spot! But I couldn't dwell on it.

I had been happy with my contribution in training, but I had had a long lay-off and not played much prior to the tour. I had played a handful of Magners League games for the Scarlets and enjoyed a mixed bag of results as we tried to secure Heineken Cup qualification for the following season, and I had been pretty happy with my form, but the Lions is another level altogether. Straight away I could feel that the opposition were determined to throw everything at us. When you tour with the Lions, it becomes very clear early on that you aren't just playing a rugby team but the whole country you're touring. While the Lions tour happens every four years for players from Britain and Ireland, it is a once-in-a-lifetime chance for the men on the opposite side. The Lions only visit every 12 years, so the teams we played against wanted to make their own bit of history.

After my initial cock-up, I settled in pretty quickly and soon found my rhythm against the Golden Lions. We had a good variety in our game and switched the focus of attack quite a bit and didn't keep attacking the same place. We asked questions of them, and that is what you want to do. We played very smart rugby against that side. I was lucky because I had played for Wales with Mike Phillips, who was at scrum-half, and Jamie Roberts, who was at inside centre, and we were on the same wavelength. The whole back line gelled very quickly. Things had gone well in training, but you never know how things are really going to work in the pressure-cooker atmosphere of a game. With Tommy Bowe, who has great hands, and Brian O'Driscoll, who is just a class act, we played with a great mix of pace and power. The back line really complemented each other nicely and I saw my job as being to get the best out of the players around me. Playing alongside someone like Brian was a real revelation. He has a great rugby brain and is very vocal on the pitch, and it was great to bounce ideas off him out in the middle. He lets you know who is marking him and what defensive policy he thinks the opposition are playing. You can do all the homework and analysis in the world, but you still have to react to what you are facing on the pitch. When you have someone like Brian in your side, giving you quality information, and who has the ability to interpret what is going on around him, it really bodes well for a game. Jamie and Brian really clicked as a centre pair and it became pretty obvious what I had to do to get the best out of them. The home side were petrified every time one of them got the ball. I made sure I gave them the ball as often as I could, with some space to wreak havoc. We knew we had to ask some big questions of their defence, but if we put them under pressure early on and forced them to make decisions, we knew the game would open up for us. We scored ten tries and ran out 74–10 winners. I landed eight out of nine kicks at goal and came off the field having enjoyed the whole experience and feeling satisfied at a job well done.

I wasn't selected for the next two games and missed the narrow 26–24 victory over the Cheetahs in Bloemfontein and the comfortable 39–3 win over the Sharks in Durban. We were still unbeaten. I was selected for my second game of the tour against Western Province at Newlands. The game ended up being a real comedy of errors. Cape Town had been hit by a storm and the wind and the rain made it almost impossible to play any real rugby. During our pre-match run-out, the tackle bags were rolling around Newlands and the ball was like a bar of soap. Trying to catch the thing was almost impossible. I knew straight away that we were going to be in for a long afternoon and that the weather would be a great leveller for both sides. Western Province would certainly have welcomed the conditions, but it meant we had to tailor our approach. The message was pretty clear about getting the job done and getting out of there. We did that and managed to get a 26–23 win. We were now five wins out of five.

The coaches, who had kept their cards very close to their chests regarding selection, split the tour party for the first time after that game. Geech explained why he didn't want to take the whole squad to Port Elizabeth and told us he had selected 12 players to fly to Durban to prepare for the first Test. I was lucky enough to be one of those players. It was the first time any of the squad could really see how selection was shaping up for the first Test. So, while the rest of the boys went to face the Southern Kings, we were packed off to Durban. I was still wondering if we had really done enough, but that was when the magnitude of what we were about to do hit home.

The boys got a 20–8 victory over the Southern Kings, but the ferocity of the home side's performance certainly focused the minds of the dozen players in Durban. You always know what you are going to get when you play the Springboks, and that is a massive physical battle and confrontation. They are probably the most physical rugby side in the world and they really enjoy that area of the game because they are good at it. We knew we had to match them physically, but the bottom line was that we couldn't let that become our only priority and had to remember what we were good at and what our strengths were.

With the Test series about to begin and the hype in South Africa going into overdrive, and the hordes of Lions fans starting to arrive, the controversy over the poor ticket sales for the early tour reared its ugly head. As a player, during the 80 minutes of the game, the crowd is not really something you notice because you are focused on what is happening in front of you on the field. The whole of the tour party had noticed the crowds hadn't been great and the stadiums had been half-empty, but it was only afterwards that we discovered that the price of watching the Lions was three times more expensive than a Tri-Nations game. That is a disgrace, really, when you think the Lions were in South Africa for the first time in 12 years, were the talk of the country and were the only show in town. You would have thought they would have wanted to fill the stadiums for all of the games, not just the Test series.

To finally get the nod and be told I was wearing the number 10 shirt for the Lions in the first Test was very humbling and daunting. I knew we had a hell of a job to do but appreciated I had completed the second step to being a Lion. First, you get on the tour. Second, you get in the Test side. All we had to do was win a Test series now.

You need form to get selected for a Lions tour, but the form that gets you selected throughout the season means nothing when you are actually on tour. It is all about the here and now, and that is all that counts. There is no time to find your feet, settle in or find your rhythm. You have to play to your best there and then. Coaches may respect what they have seen you do on the pitch all season, but when you are on tour, it's all about what they get from you in a one-on-one situation in training that counts and convinces them to select you for games and ultimately the Test matches. That is what makes the Lions so unique. It's not a place to develop players or try out new ideas. It's about doing everything to the very highest level with the best players.

It became very clear during training sessions and team meetings what the coaches were looking for. They wanted real leaders, players who would bring something more to the table than just their ability on the pitch, who would add a little extra to the squad. They wanted players with a rugby brain who could do their own job and bring out the best in those around them, who would implement the game plan they wanted. I was one of the lucky ones.

The first Test was a major disappointment for us. We started badly and left ourselves a mountain to climb for the rest of the series. We were 19–7 down at half-time, though we did come back and played most of the rugby in the second half. The Boks were pretty conservative, but they could afford to be because they were in the driving seat. We lost 26–21 and, despite being slow out of the blocks, we had found some real momentum. If we'd had more time on the clock, we might even have won, but we made too many mistakes and our execution over the whole 80 minutes wasn't good enough.

Phil Vickery, the England and Wasps prop, was the target of a barrage of criticism following the first Test after our scrum had been targeted by the Springboks. We had been pretty much under pressure in that facet of play for all of the first half of the game. Vicks is a great character and a real rugby warrior, and we could all see he was hurting after what had happened to him. For props in the scrum, where you are up against another prop, it is personal. He had been beaten by his opposite number, but I had huge admiration for him for the way he handled the situation. He could easily have disappeared and decided his tour was over there and then, but he didn't, and two weeks later in the third Test he redeemed himself with a towering display in the scrum. He is a mentally tough character, and you want guys like that in the trenches alongside you.

Despite losing the first Test, we still felt we could win the Test series. We knew we had our backs to the wall and looked at everything in the game. We knew that we had finished the stronger side and that when we had had the ball we had caused the Boks problems. We knew we didn't have to make too many changes to our game plan, but in the second Test we had to do what we had done for 40 minutes in the second half for the full 80 minutes. We just had to play, and couldn't afford to go into our shells or be scared and chance our arms. We had to pose them problems, something we had only done in the second half in the first Test. The coaches made it very clear that they wanted us to play rugby from the first minute. I was told to play very flat, to put some width on the ball early and to get us into the game and on the front foot. We were not going to play conservative rugby; we were going to attack them.

The second Test in Pretoria was legalised brutality. It was the most savage game of rugby I have ever played in. If the first Test was two boxers seeing what the other had and probing for openings and weaknesses, the second Test was a full-on toe-to-toe slug-fest, with both sides trying to knock the other out. Nobody took a backward step. The media hype in the week had gone up another level and nervous excitement was coursing through our veins come kick-off. It was now or never. Do or die time.

My kick-off wasn't the greatest to start the match, but it was overshadowed by an incident that would probably decide the Test series and become the controversy of the tour. I tried to get the ball to hang in the air a bit longer and clear the Boks' lifting pods, who were waiting to receive the ball, so our pack could really challenge for it. I kicked it, but it didn't clear those lifting pods. They got a rolling maul going and started to move up the field with some real momentum. I dropped back to deep right wing, knowing I had put my own pack under pressure. The home crowd were roaring the

Boks on as they rumbled upfield with a very good rolling maul, but then it collapsed. Gethin Jenkins, quick as a flash, turned around to me with his hands in the air, effectively asking me: what kind of a kick was that? I tried to play dumb. Meanwhile, Schalk Burger had been shown the yellow card – in the first minute of the second Test. I only found out later, after the game was over, that he'd been sin-binned for eye-gouging.

I have met Schalk and played against him many times. He is one of the good guys and doesn't have a reputation for being a dirty player, but you cannot condone what he did to Luke Fitzgerald. There is no question he should have been shown a red card, because what he did was inexcusable. I don't know if he got caught up with the emotion of winning his 50th cap, but the Boks should have played the rest of the game with 14 men. Both sides knew what was at stake and there was stuff going on all over the pitch. The Boks wanted to bully us out of the game and we just weren't going to take a step backwards and allow them to do that. I even managed to have my moment with Bismarck du Plessis, the Springbok hooker, when he came for me after the referee had already blown his whistle for a break in play. He tackled me from behind while I was picking up the ball. I was fuming and just threw the ball at him, and it hit him in the face. It was a childish thing to do, but I got a lot of satisfaction from it!

We started the second Test with real attitude and after seven minutes scored the first try of the game. We had played with real pace and good variety, but the lungs were really burning badly. I did take some stick off the Welsh boys for the pass out of the back door for Rob Kearney's try to give us a 10–0 lead early in the game. They claimed they had played with me for nearly ten years and never seen me try a pass like that and that I had saved my best for the Lions! But I had seen Bryan Habana, the Springboks wing, out of the corner of my eye and I knew he always came in looking for the tackle when he defended, so I managed to get the ball away and Rob did all the real work for the try. We had made a perfect start, and had caught the world champions out with our intensity, attitude and skill, and went in 16–8 ahead at half-time.

South Africa showed what a good side they are in the second half, when they changed their approach and played with much more width and moved the ball through the hand. The battle of the breakdown was massive, as it had been all tour, but the fact the scrums became uncontested for the last 35 minutes of the second Test was a massive blow for us because our scrum had been a strong part of our game in the first half. Gethin, Matthew Rees and Adam Jones had done a great job, giving us a solid platform to play from and putting the Boks under real pressure; when the scrums became null and void, it had a massive knock-on effect. It meant the Boks' back row were fresher than they would have been; they could detach from the scrum much more quickly and didn't have to push at all come scrum time. It meant they could just run around the park, while their front five were fresher because they weren't under pressure and didn't have to work at the scrum either. It was a massive bonus for them; it meant they could carry the ball and hit rucks with the extra energy we could have taken away from them at the scrum. It allowed them to recharge their batteries and come back at us in the second half. It was the turning point of the game, and the Test series.

Big games turn on little things and moments that people aren't always aware of. For example, there was one decision I made towards the end of the first half that would seem insignificant to some. There was one minute and thirty seconds until half-time and I called an attacking move from a scrum around the halfway line. We did the move well, but were penalised for crossing and François Steyn, who has a massive boot on him, smashed the penalty over from miles out. It made the score 16–8 instead of 16–5 as both sides went into their respective dressing-rooms. With hindsight, should I have kicked to the corner for the lineout? Had I done that, we wouldn't have conceded those three points. All conjecture now, but little things like that matter in big games.

The Boks hadn't got close to our line for ten minutes before

Steyn converted the penalty and they didn't look like scoring a try against us, so the psychological edge would have been with us, while they would have been asking themselves some real questions in their dressing-room at the break. Being a fly-half is all about game-management and being smart and aware of everything around you, including the clock. My mindset will always be to play, but sometimes you have to weigh up your options. You cannot always attack and be idealistic on the pitch. It's the biggest lesson I have learned. Test match rugby is all about winning – winning is everything. I realise more and more that the opportunities to nail the big games are getting rarer, but it's essential to be able to recognise those moments when they come along. They aren't always somebody scoring a try or landing a kick.

During the second half, I landed a couple of kicks to keep us in the lead, but our hosts really came after us and lifted the intensity to another level. We lost Adam, Gethin, Jamie and Brian to injury in the second half, and Tommy and I moved to the centre, while Rog came on at fly-half. It was all hands to the pumps. We were getting battered physically and the altitude had started to really kick in as they began to claw their way back into the contest. We had led all game until Jaque Fourie crashed over and through Rog in the corner for the try. Morne Steyn converted to make it 25–23 to our hosts before I had a chance to level the scores with three minutes still on the clock.

I had been high tackled and we were awarded a penalty on the touchline at Loftus Versfeld. People always ask me what goes through my mind in a high-pressure moment like that during a game, but the answer is always the same. I just go through my tried-and-tested routine and think of the 'opportunity' I have been given; I don't worry about the 'outcome'. Having someone like Neil Jenkins, former world points record holder, always with you out on the pitch as a water-carrier is a constant reminder of the standards I have to hit as a goal-kicker.

My kicking routine is always the same. I place the tee, then place the ball at an angle on top of that tee. Stand up, four steps back in a straight line, two and a half steps to the left and aim towards the posts, taking into consideration any wind, but never aiming outside the posts. I have a few trigger phrases, such as 'through the ball' and 'keep square', and when I am ready I step up and kick the ball. There is no secret to goal-kicking: it is all about practice and visualisation. I just focus on the process. The delight or disappointment of the crowd doesn't even enter my head because I am so engrossed in what I am trying to do on the field. If I thought of the consequences of missing a kick – not being selected for the next game and, more importantly, losing the game – I would never step up to take a kick!

The night before every game I visualise what I will do, and the ball sailing through the posts. The morning of a game I do the same. My brain is usually in overdrive, thinking about the game and the team's game plan on the morning of every match. That is probably the most intense time for me before every game, and the most stressful. When the team bus gets to the ground, I usually get changed quickly and go through my kicking routine on the field and get myself in the zone. Any nerves, or anything like that, are usually gone by this point.

I have learnt, too, that a successful or failed kick doesn't always mean victory or defeat. The opposition could still score and win the game, whether my kick has been successful or not. I put it straight out of my mind and focus on what I have to do next. You are really living in the moment and cannot think: 'I have just won or lost the game.' You cannot dwell on the fact you have missed your previous three shots at goal before you step up to kick. I certainly don't concentrate on what the score is and just focus on getting my routine right. If I do that, I will convert the kick.

I did all of that at Loftus Versfeld before the penalty to level the second Test 25–25 with three minutes to go, but was very much aware there was still enough time for the Boks to come back at us and still clinch the victory, and with it the Test series.

What happened next was a prime example of how brutal and ruthless professional sport, let alone professional rugby, can be. Rog, who had been the Grand Slam hero for Ireland a few months earlier with his last-ditch drop goal, became the so-called pantomime villain of the contest. Rog had already seen Fourie smash through him for a try, but then tackled scrum-half Fourie du Preez in the air and the Boks were awarded a penalty I knew they would convert. Rog, who had been out on his feet and had a nasty cut around his eye after Fourie's try, was blamed for 'a moment of madness' that cost us the game and the Test series. I don't believe that and would never apportion blame to one player. People do pinpoint certain instances where they believe a game is won or lost, but, as a player, I always look at the bigger picture. Losing our two props and two centres to injury had a much bigger impact on the Lions in that Test than anything. When Gethin, Adam, Brian and Jamie went off, we lost our momentum and it swung to the Boks.

Morne Steyn, the replacement fly-half, who was on his home ground and had been part of the Blue Bulls side that had beaten the Waikato Chiefs 61–17 in the Super 14 final in Pretoria, landed the penalty to clinch the victory and the Test series. I knew before he had even teed the ball up that he was going to convert it. The majority of the Boks were from the Blue Bulls franchise and you could see they were so comfortable playing in Pretoria. There were just no unknowns or imponderables for them to consider before or during the game. Steyn got the kick and it was, quite literally, game over. All of us were distraught after the final whistle and Loftus was a pretty lonely place to be.

The dressing-room was full of battered and bruised bodies. It was like an accident and emergency room with the silence of a morgue. We had lost the game and the Test series. Gethin had reopened stitches he had had above his eye in the first Test and had another gash across his forehead, which also required stitches, and he had smashed his cheekbone. He was in a right mess. Adam had dislocated his shoulder; Tommy had a problem with his elbow;

Jamie had damaged his wrist; Brian had concussion; and Rog had a gash around his eye. We were not a pretty sight. All in all, five players – Adam Jones, Gethin, Tommy, Brian and Jamie – went to hospital after that game. It had been a brutal confrontation and we had the physical and mental scars to prove it.

The following Sunday in the hotel was very quiet and low-key. People were walking around in a daze and everybody was in a very reflective mood. Playing the third Test was the last thing on anybody's mind. But this was when the coaches showed how very smart they were and gave us all a couple of days off. Some of the boys went on a safari, but I chose to stay behind and give myself time to recover from all our bumps and bruises. We didn't train at all until the Wednesday before the third Test and felt re-energised for the challenge ahead, though our first training session left a lot to be desired. The back line, without Jamie and Brian, was a new-look one and we were very ropey, to say the least. We ran moves and our timing was awful. It took us three occasions to get one simple move right. The omens weren't good. We looked like a side that had lost a game and a Test series the previous weekend.

The coaches, to their credit, didn't hammer us on the training pitch and instead slowly brought us back to the boil. The tendency for most coaches is to work their players harder after a defeat, but the Lions coaches did the opposite and made sure we all wanted to play in the third Test.

Geech and Gats both delivered superb speeches about why we were playing rugby and why we were in South Africa. The sight of Gats with a Lions shirt above his shoulder talking about players who would never wear this jersey again was inspirational stuff. He mentioned my name as one of those players who would never wear a Lions shirt again and it hit home how important the game was for me. I did collar him after the game and say, 'Cheers for mentioning my name, Gats. I had a flickering light at the end of the tunnel about making Australia in four years' time, but you put it out before this game!' We had a good laugh about it afterwards.

Everybody expected us to get hammered in the third Test in Ellis Park because we had lost the Test series. People thought because we had lost the Test series that we might as well go home, but it was really easy to get right for the game mentally. How did we get motivated for the game? Simple, we were playing for the Lions, the biggest honour you can have in your career. We were about to pull on a Lions Test jersey and all of us understood how special that was. There were players in the side for the third Test who had been given the chance to wear the Lions jersey in a Test match. It only happens every four years. Our biggest problem was getting our rugby preparation right in only two training sessions, but we tried to keep it simple and had real faith in what we were doing, and in each other. All of the Boks wore a 'Justice 4 Bakkies' armband for the third Test, but it didn't mean anything to the Lions and we didn't see it as an insult, or anything like that. It was totally irrelevant to us and didn't affect us at all.

My only regret about the Test series, and it gnaws away at me now, is that perhaps we didn't really express ourselves in the first Test in Durban. But why didn't we? Were we too reluctant to have a real go at them because there was so much at stake? I think so, and that is a sad thing to say. I am not blaming anybody else; I have asked myself whether I was too conservative, whether I took enough risks in that first half, whether I was too concerned with not making mistakes rather than winning. We lost it anyway, but only after we had really chanced our arm in the second half because we had no option. And we did cause them all sorts of problems. If we had played like that for the whole 80 minutes, would we have won the first Test and the Test series? Who knows? Hindsight is a wonderful thing. We didn't make many mistakes in that first half, but we didn't really take any risks or show them what we were capable of, and we certainly didn't throw the kitchen sink at them.

Looking back, the Test series had it all. Both sides played some really good rugby and the mix of power and skill needed in the Test match arena was there. It wasn't a Test series dominated by the boot and all the players tried to show off their respective skills. I can remember a banana kick by Fourie du Preez in the second Test that was ridiculously skilful, and it landed perfectly for his wing. If I had been in the crowd, I would have stood up and applauded what I had just seen. It was an outrageous example of the quality in both sides. They had done their homework, analysed how we defended, and had spotted a weakness and exploited it. Du Preez's skill was just something nobody could have defended against.

Shane Williams showed what a class act he is in the third Test. He was brilliant. He scored two tries and let us see what a great finisher he is – and why he was World Player of the Year and Wales's record try-scorer. We had finished on a high and I had finally tasted victory in a Lions Test match.

The thought of coming home at the end of another 3–0 whitewash had been in the back of my mind, but thankfully we had avoided that and the inevitable post-mortem about the future of the Lions. The whole tour had been a great experience, but a Lions tour is all about winning the Test series, something we hadn't done. We were close, but there was no cigar at the end of the three matches for the class of 2009. We had managed a win at Ellis Park, one of the great rugby grounds of the world, and it was a good way to end the trip.

As I have got older, I have become more and more aware of the knock-on effect of losing on my teammates, coaches and, of course, supporters. That's before I even think about how important the business of winning is to the commercial success of a team. Defeat can tarnish the reputation of all of those who have worked so hard on the field and off it. It took a while for the penny to drop about the ramifications of victory, but especially defeat. I can watch a football game and enjoy it and forget it almost straight away, just like any fan. But as a player who is involved with rugby I take all the emotions of the game – the good, the bad and the ugly – on board if I have lost. I carry it around with me and sometimes it lasts for a whole week. I have got better at dealing with defeat, but it is still there.

From a Welsh perspective, I look back on the tour and think it can only be good for Wales. Yes, we had lost some players to injury, but we had held our own in a very physical Test series, against the most physical side in the world. Some of the Welsh boys were frontline players for the Lions and we finally know what it takes to beat the Boks in their own backyard, something I had never experienced before. We conducted ourselves well and really gave something to the environment, and I feel it can only be good for Welsh rugby. We made a big contribution and I cannot emphasise how important that was for the 2009 Lions. We weren't a little clique of Welshmen, and made sure everybody was aware of what we did with Wales and why we thought it worked. There were no agendas; we all wanted the Lions to achieve the impossible dream. We opened the doors and didn't hide any information or keep anything back. The big question for every player and coach is: how much knowledge do you give away? Do you want everybody to know your moves and patterns and why you do certain things on the field at certain times during a game? We were open and gave it all away for the Lions' cause and I feel that is the way it should be.

There was a lot of debate about having so many Welsh coaches with the Lions, along with the fear that Warren, Shaun and Rob could find themselves compromised when they came back to their day jobs with Wales. Graham Henry, of course, has said he suffered after the 2001 Lions tour to Australia because certain Welsh players weren't selected for the tour or the Test side. But this is a very different Welsh squad from back then and I don't envisage any problems at all. In fact, I can only see the fact that three of our coaches were involved as beneficial for Wales. The Welsh players did themselves justice in South Africa and that will be massive for us over the next few years. There are now Welsh players who know what it takes to beat the world champions, and that winning mentality becomes a habit. Wales are now a highly competitive team and we all realise Test match rugby is all about winning.

There has been a lot of talk about the viability of the Lions concept since the tour and how important it is that the Lions win a Test series because they haven't won one since 1997. All sorts of things have been suggested, like a longer tour, longer preparation time and even that an extended Lions squad should be selected and train together during the season, building to a Lions tour. For the 2012 Olympics in London, potential star athletes have already been identified and are being groomed to compete in the event, but I don't think the same approach will ever work for the Lions. I believe the Lions would lose their magic if that happened – and you mess with the Lions at your peril. It is a truly unique concept in any sport in the world. Four countries come together in one team every four years to try and achieve the impossible. The best of the best, the cream of the crop try to become a team in two months, then try to become a successful one, then try to beat the three best teams in the world – Australia, New Zealand and South Africa – on their home patch. History tells us that the Lions aren't always successful – they have only won four Test series – but that is what makes being a successful Lion so special. A Lions tour, if it is done correctly, represents all the good things about rugby. The fact that it is so at odds with professional rugby only adds to its appeal.

The British and Irish Lions lie dormant for three and a half years and then suddenly dominate everything. They come alive and capture the imagination of everyone. Coaches will always tell you it takes two or three years to build a team, but you have only two months to do exactly that with the Lions. The Test side changes dramatically over the three weeks of the Test series, mainly due to injury and suspensions, and you have next to no time to prepare a team. Nobody knows what style of play the Lions will adopt or who will emerge as the stars of the team. It all adds to the aura of the Lions. It is an impossible challenge and I wouldn't change it at all.

If there is a moment that sums up the 2009 Lions, and probably the Lions ethos, for me, it wouldn't be a victory, a try or even a successful kick, but the huddle on the pitch after the victory in the third Test in Ellis Park. The players, coaches, physios, administration staff, doctors and security staff were all together, and it was great. It summed up what being in the Lions is all about. It was a strange, sad and profound moment because I will never play or spend time with some of those people again. We all knew we wouldn't be together again, but we had done our best, given it everything and could all look ourselves in the mirror after the 2009 tour.

CHAPTER 14

LIFE AFTER RUGBY

The whole point of rugby is that it is, first and foremost,
a state of mind, a spirit.

– Jean-Pierre Rives, French rugby legend

The end of my career is now much closer than the start of it and pretty soon I will probably have to get a proper job and leave behind the sheltered and cosseted life of professional rugby. Not bad for a thirty-something! I have never seen rugby as a job in the normal sense of the word. I have been very well rewarded for what I have done and have no regrets whatsoever. It has been a fantastic journey, with as many highs as lows, but that is life. Saying that, I do wish I had really listened and paid attention to some of the advice I was given by some great coaches over the years. The likes of Graham Henry, Steve Hansen and Scott Johnson were spot on about so many things about the game – so many things about *my* game. I was young, too stubborn and too proud to admit they were right, but as I have become older and wiser I have realised they were right about so many things. I just wish I had realised it at the time and listened more.

People involved in sport always say they will know when to call it a day, and retired sportspeople always claim they can almost pinpoint the day they've had enough. I hope that happens to me. I would hate to go on too long, but I have to say I am enjoying my rugby more than ever at the moment. My long-term aim is to play in a fourth World Cup for Wales, in New Zealand in 2011, but I have learnt never to look too far ahead. Rugby has a nasty way of biting you on the backside just when you think you have made it or have started to make big plans to do this or that. The great irony of sport is that just when you are at your peak mentally and have so much experience behind you, it is the body that gives way. I know this has happened to so many athletes, not just rugby players. You have finally sussed the game out, know all the pitfalls and have all the experience in the world to call on, but physically you just cannot deliver any more. I just hope I know when to call it a day and don't try to fight the inevitable. I won't miss the ice-baths or the strict discipline you need to be a professional player, but I will miss the banter and the adrenaline rush before a game. Most importantly, I will miss the 80 minutes on the pitch. There is still nothing quite like it.

I have to admit the prospect of a life without rugby and my teammates and the buzz of game-day does scare me. It has been such a big part of my life, but there is also a part of me that is relishing the chance to do things my rugby career has stopped me from doing. I don't know the number of family occasions or friends' engagement parties or weddings I have missed over the years due to my rugby commitments. I would never complain or moan about that, but it will be good to actually be there for the special occasions in my friends' and family's lives.

Dwayne Peel and I have a new restaurant opening in Llanelli in the next year or so and that has proved to be a really good project to get involved in. We are part of a firm called Bendigo Boys, which includes Simon Wright, the food critic, and Robert Williams, a successful businessman and loyal supporter of the Scarlets. I am afraid to say I know very little about the restaurant trade, apart from the fact I love to eat out, so it has been an eye-opener but something I really want to get involved in. We are planning for 100 covers – and you will be glad to know I will *not* be in the kitchen. Nor will Peely, for that matter!

Then, of course, there is Ski Sunday, the racehorse run by the big-money Scarlets consortium of Simon Easterby, Regan King, former Scarlets chief executive Stuart Gallacher and myself! I wish. To be honest, I know next to nothing about horse-racing and defer on all matters to Easters and Reg. They have all the lingo off pat and both really fancy themselves as the next J.P. McManus. Going to the races is a really good way to get away from rugby and is always a good day out. Watching a horse you own run at an event such as Cheltenham, even for a novice like me, is spine-tingling. I have found myself studying form, and horse-training does fascinate me, although I am no Michael Owen and don't plan to buy or run my own horse-race stable or anything like that. Our trainer, Tim Vaughan, always gives us an insight into what he has been doing with the Ski and the psychology he uses to get the horse in the right mood to perform. I have to say, some of what he does is remarkably similar to the ploys coaches use to get the best out of their players! I am not a great gambler – you can take the boy out of West Wales, but you cannot take West Wales out of the boy! I am what the Welsh call a typical 'Cardi' and don't part with money easily – and I am glad I am not. Why? Because I am a terrible tipster! But it's a good day out and I thoroughly enjoy it.

People have been kind enough to say I should consider becoming some kind of coach when my career is over, and there is a certain attraction to being a kicking or skills coach, but it's not something I have considered too deeply. The thought of giving something back to the game and helping young players does appeal to me, but it's not a burning desire at the moment. I have given up my weekends, travelling or playing rugby, for most of my adult life and I want to do all the things everybody else does on a weekend for a while.

When my career does come to its inevitable end, I have promised myself some time away from the game. Professional rugby is 24/7. It is a lifestyle, more than a job. For a while I do want to experience normal life, something I have never really done. Having free weekends and spending time with Gwen, my family and my friends is something I am determined to do. One of the great perks of being a rugby player is that I have had the opportunity to travel the world and have met some great people along the way. I am very aware that my rugby career has opened doors for me and that I have been very, very lucky; now I would like to travel more and just take in places and countries I have probably rushed through before and just relax and enjoy the company of some of the good people I have had the good fortune to meet over the years.

All of that, of course, is for the future. Until then, I have a rugby career and am determined to make the most of the time I have left in the game. There are so many challenges on the horizon with the Scarlets and Wales. The Scarlets is a side and an organisation in transition, and I want to play my part in getting them back to where they should be on the European stage. The place has given me so much – I want to give something back and play whatever role I can in making sure we live up to our great tradition and proud history.

I have been lucky enough to be part of the current Wales set-up, under Warren Gatland, Shaun Edwards and Rob Howley, and I want to stay there. Their arrival kicked everybody out of their comfort zone and I can only see good things for the national side with them at the helm. They challenge all the players all the time and that is what you want as a senior pro; there is nothing worse than feeling you aren't learning anything or being pushed to fulfil your potential. Warren has built a 'no excuses' environment and we have a group of players who can achieve anything they want to, if they put their minds to it.

Rugby has given me a great life. It has tested me and, I would like to think, brought out the best in me. I have made more mistakes than I care to remember, but I would like to think I have always tried to learn from them. I have definitely thought too deeply about the game, but then I have always believed rugby, despite players getting bigger and stronger, is still a thinking man's game.

VOICES FROM THE BACK OF THE BUS
TALL TALES AND HOARY STORIES FROM
RUGBY'S REAL HEROES

STEWART McKINNEY

ISBN 9781845965440
AVAILABLE NOW
£16.99 (HARDBACK)

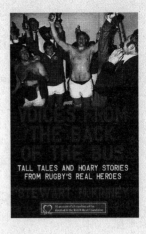

Voices from the Back of the Bus provides a rare behind-the-scenes look at international rugby at the height of a golden period.

Recounted with genuine warmth and much humour, over a hundred players – many of them British and Irish Lions – recall the scrapes, the games, the laughs, the glory and the gritty reality of the pre-professional game.

Former Lion Stewart McKinney has collected priceless recollections of the glory days from an unprecedented number of legendary rugby names. The all-star cast includes: from England, Peter Wheeler, Jeff Probyn, Andy Ripley and Mickey Skinner; from Ireland, Willie John McBride and Moss Keane; from Wales, Gareth Edwards, Phil Bennett and Mervyn Davies; and from Scotland, Andy Irvine and Ian McLauchlan, with contributions also made from New Zealand and South African rugby stars.

Packed with true rugby tales from the days when men played purely for the love of the game and of their nation, and multimillion-pound contracts and sponsorship deals were unheard of, *Voices from the Back of the Bus* is a refreshing, revealing and often hilarious collection that will inspire sports fans of all generations.

Available from all good bookshops, mainstreampublishing.com and rbooks.co.uk

NOBODY BEATS US
THE INSIDE STORY OF THE 1970s
WALES RUGBY TEAM

DAVID TOSSELL

ISBN 9781845964429
AVAILABLE NOW
£16.99 (HARDBACK)

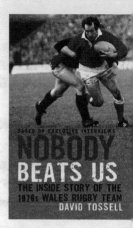

'Tossell is an accomplished writer' – *Independent on Sunday*

In the 1970s, an age long before World Cups, rugby union to the British public meant Bill McLaren, rude songs and, most of all, Wales. Between 1969 and 1979, the men in red shirts won or shared eight Five Nations Championships, including three Grand Slams and six Triple Crowns.

But the mere facts resonate less than the enduring images of the precision of Gareth Edwards, the sublime touch of Barry John, the sidesteps of Gerald Davies and Phil Bennett, the courage of J.P.R. Williams, and the forward power of the Pontypool Front Row and 'Merv the Swerve' Davies.

To the land of their fathers, these Welsh heroes represented pride and conquest at a time when the decline of the province's traditional coal and steel industries was sending thousands to the dole queue and threatening the fabric of local communities. Yet the achievements of those players transcended their homeland and extended beyond mere rugby fans.

In *Nobody Beats Us*, David Tossell, who spent the '70s as a schoolboy scrum-half trying to perfect the Gareth Edwards reverse pass, interviews many of the key figures of a golden age of Welsh rugby and vividly recreates an unforgettable sporting era.

SEEING RED
TWELVE TUMULTUOUS YEARS
IN WELSH RUGBY

ALUN CARTER WITH NICK BISHOP

ISBN 9781845964825
AVAILABLE NOW
£7.99 (PAPERBACK)

'Carter wields a sharp pen, and draws blood from a number of key figures he feels were flawed . . . explosive . . . revelatory' – Book of the Week, *Independent on Sunday*

Alun Carter experienced the highs and lows of the Wales national rugby squad throughout his 12 years working for the WRU. During this time, he saw a number of high-profile coaches come and go, and in *Seeing Red* he delivers a brutally honest account of what it was like to work with each of them.

Carter does not shy away from controversy, and he pulls no punches in his assessment of the rift between Graham Henry and Sir Clive Woodward, the personal and political situation that led to Mike Ruddock losing his job, and the difficulty of handling the group dynamics within the national squad.

Winner of best rugby book at the 2009 British Sports Book Awards, *Seeing Red* provides a warts-and-all account of more than a decade of Welsh rugby and is packed with revelations, exclusive contributions and untold stories that will intrigue and delight all fans of the sport.